FAVOURITE HYMNS

104 Easy-to-play arrangements
for keyboard by Alan Ridout

Kevin
Mayhew

We hope you enjoy the music in this book. Further copies are available
from your local music shop or Christian bookshop.

In case of difficulty, please contact the publisher direct by writing to:

The Sales Department
KEVIN MAYHEW LTD
Buxhall
Stowmarket
Suffolk
IP14 3DJ

Phone 01449 737978
Fax 01449 737834
E-mail info@kevinmayhew.com

Please ask for our complete catalogue of outstanding Church Music.

First published in Great Britain in 1994 by Kevin Mayhew Ltd.

This edition © Copyright 1998 Kevin Mayhew Ltd.

ISBN 1 84003 291 X
ISMN M 57004 452 8
Catalogue No: 1400201

1 2 3 4 5 6 7 8 9

Front cover illustration by Karen Perrins.
Cover designed by Jaquetta Sergeant.

Index of First Lines

1 Abide with me

1. A - bide with me; fast falls the ev - en - tide: the dark- ness deep - ens; Lord, with me a - bide: when o - ther help - ers fail, and com-forts flee, help of the help-less, O a - bide with me.

2. Swift to its close ebbs out life's little day,
   earth's joys grow dim, its glories pass away;
   change and decay in all round I see:
   O thou who changest not, abide with me.

3. I need thy presence every passing hour;
   what but thy grace can foil the tempter's power?
   Who like thyself my guide and stay can be?
   Through cloud and sunshine, Lord, abide with me.

4. I fear no foe with thee at hand to bless;
   ills have no weight, and tears no bitterness.
   Where is death's sting? Where, grave, thy victory?
   I triumph still, if thou abide with me.

5. Hold thou thy cross before my closing eyes;
   shine through the gloom, and point me to the skies:
   heaven's morning breaks, and earth's vain shadows flee;
   in life, in death, O Lord, abide with me.

EVENTIDE 10 10. 10 10.
Text: Henry Francis Lyte (1793-1847) Music: William Henry Monk (1823-1889)

2 All creatures of our God and King

2. Thou rushing wind that art so strong,
   ye clouds that sail in heaven along,
   O praise him, alleluia.
   Thou rising morn, in praise rejoice,
   ye lights of evening, find a voice;

3. Thou flowing water, pure and clear,
   make music for thy Lord to hear,
   alleluia, alleluia.
   Thou fire so masterful and bright,
   that givest man both warmth and light:

4. Dear mother earth, who day by day
   unfoldest blessings on our way,
   O praise him, alleluia.
   The flowers and fruits that in thee grow,
   let them his glory also show:

5. And all ye men of tender heart,
   forgiving others, take your part,
   O sing ye alleluia.
   Ye who long pain and sorrow bear,
   praise God and on him cast your care:

6. And thou, most kind and gentle death,
   waiting to hush our latest breath,
   O praise him, alleluia.
   Thou leadest home the child of God,
   and Christ our Lord the way hath trod:

7. Let all things their Creator bless,
   and worship him in humbleness;
   O praise him, alleluia.
   Praise, praise the Father, praise the Son,
   and praise the Spirit, three in one;

LASST UNS ERFREUEN 8 8. 4 4. 8 8.
Text: William Henry Draper (1855-1933)   Melody from *Geistliche Kirchengesäng,* Cologne (1623)

3 All glory, laud and honour

Chorus
All glo-ry, laud and ho-nour to thee, Re-deem-er, King, to

whom the lips of child-ren made sweet ho-san-nas ring. 1. Thou
Verse
Fine

art the King of Is-rael, thou Da-vid's roy-al son who

in the Lord's name com-est, the King and bles-sed one.
D.C. al Fine

2. The company of angels
   are praising thee on high,
   and mortal men and all things
   created make reply:

3. The people of the Hebrews
   with palms before thee went:
   our praise and prayer and anthems
   before thee we present:

4. To thee before thy passion
   they sang their hymns of praise:
   to thee now high exalted
   our melody we raise:

5. Thou didst accept their praises:
   accept the prayers we bring,
   who in all good delightest,
   thou good and gracious King:

ST THEODULPH 7 6. 7 6. D.
Text: Theodulph of Orleans (d. 821), translated by John Mason Neale (1818-1866)
Music: Melchior Teschner (1584-1635), adapted by Johann Sebastian Bach (1685-1750)

4 All hail the power of Jesus' name!

1. All hail the power of Jesus' name! Let angels prostrate fall; bring forth the royal diadem and crown him, crown him, crown him, crown him, Lord of all.

2. Crown him, ye morning stars of light,
   who fixed this floating ball;
   now hail the strength of Israel's might,
   and crown him Lord of all.

3. Crown him, ye martyrs of your God,
   who from his altar call;
   extol the stem of Jesse's rod,
   and crown him Lord of all.

4. Ye seed of Israel's chosen race,
   ye ransomed of the fall,
   hail him who saves you by his grace,
   and crown him Lord of all.

5. Sinners, whose love can ne'er forget
   the wormwood and the gall,
   go spread your trophies at his feet,
   and crown him Lord of all.

6. Let every tribe and every tongue
   before him prostrate fall,
   and shout in universal song
   the crownèd Lord of all.

MILES LANE C. M.
Text: Edward Perronet (c. 1726-1792) Music: William Shrubsole (1760-1806)

5 All people that on earth do dwell

2. The Lord, ye know, is God indeed;
   without our aid he did us make;
   we are his folk, he doth us feed,
   and for his sheep he doth us take.

3. O enter then his gates with praise,
   approach with joy his courts unto;
   praise, laud, and bless his name always,
   for its seemly so to do.

4. For why? the Lord our God is good;
   his mercy is for every sure;
   his truth at all times firmly stood,
   and shall from age to age endure.

5. To Father, Son, and Holy Ghost,
   the God whom heaven and earth adore,
   from men and from the angel-host
   be praise and glory evermore.

OLD 100th L. M.
Text: William Kethe (d.1594) Music: Melody from the *Genevan Psalter* (1551)

6 All things bright and beautiful (1)

Chorus

All things bright and beau - ti - ful, all crea - tures great and small,

all things wise and won - der - ful, the Lord God made them all. *Fine*

Verse
1. Each

lit - tle flower that o - pens, each lit - tle bird that sings, he

made their glow - ing col - ours, he made their ti - ny wings. *D.C. al Fine*

2. The purple-headed mountain,
   the river running by,
   the sunset, and the morning
   that brightens up the sky.

3. The cold wind in the winter,
   the pleasant summer sun,
   the ripe fruits in the garden,
   he made them every one.

4. The tall trees in the greenwood,
   the meadows where we play,
   the rushes by the water
   we gather every day.

5. He gave us eyes to see them,
   and lips that we might tell
   how great is God almighty,
   who has made all things well.

ALL THINGS BRIGHT AND BEAUTIFUL 7 6. 7 6.
Text: Cecil Frances Alexander (1818-1895)
Music: Traditional English Melody

7 All things bright and beautiful (2)

2. The purple-headed mountain,
the river running by,
the sunset, and the morning
that brightens up the sky.

3. The cold wind in the winter,
the pleasant summer sun,
the ripe fruits in the garden,
he made them every one.

4. The tall trees in the greenwood,
the meadows where we play,
the rushes by the water
we gather every day.

5. He gave us eyes to see them,
and lips that we might tell
how great is God almighty,
who has made all things well.

ROYAL OAK 76.76.
Text: Cecil Frances Alexander (1818-1895)
Music: Traditional English Melody

8 All ye who seek a comfort sure

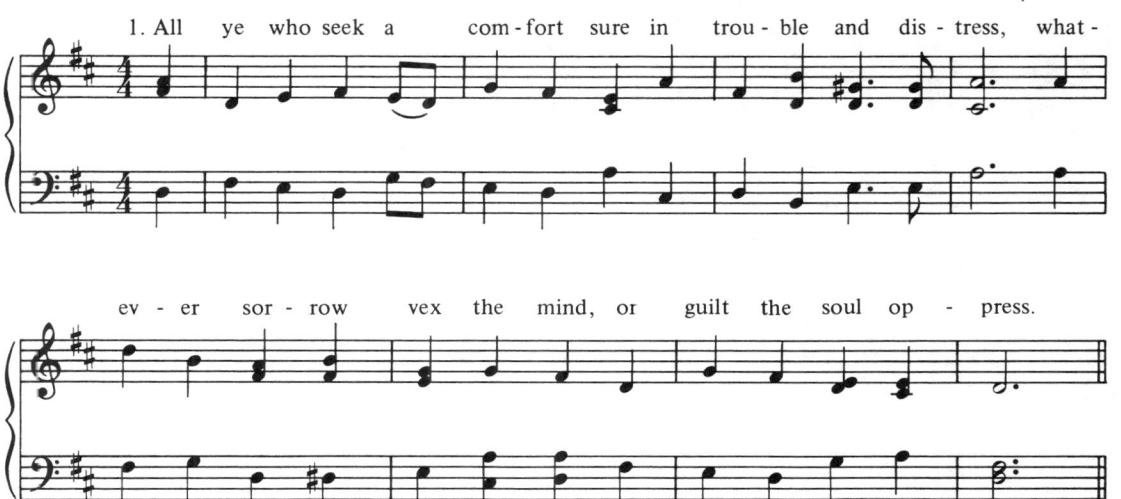

2. Jesus, who gave himself for you
   upon the cross to die,
   opens to you his sacred heart;
   O to that heart draw nigh.

3. Ye hear how kindly he invites;
   ye hear his words so blest –
   'All ye that labour come to me,
   and I will give you rest.'

4. O Jesus, joy of saints on high,
   thou hope of sinners here,
   attracted by those loving words
   to thee I lift my prayer.

5. Wash thou my wounds in that dear blood
   which forth from thee doth flow;
   new grace, new hope inspire, a new
   and better heart bestow.

ST BERNARD C. M.
Text: Translated from the Latin (18c.) by Edward Caswall (1814-1878)
Music: Adapted from a Melody in *Tochter Sion*, Cologne (1741)

9 Alleluia, give thanks

2. Spread the good news o'er all the earth.
   Jesus has died and is risen.

3. We have been crucified with Christ.
   Now we shall live forever.

4. God has proclaimed the just reward:
   life for all men, alleluia.

5. Come, let us praise the living God,
   joyfully sing to our Saviour.

Text and Music: Donald Fishel

10 Alleluia, sing to Jesus!

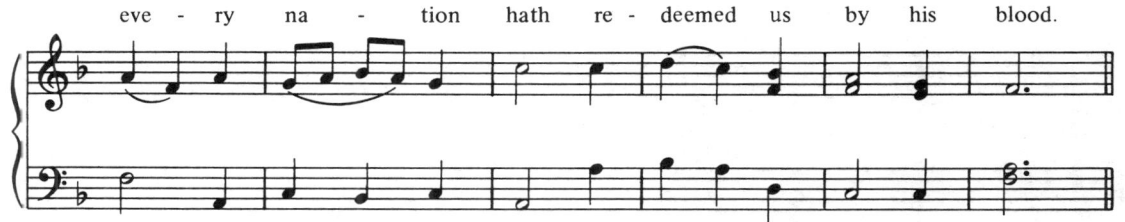

eve - ry na - tion hath re - deemed us by his blood.

2. Alleluia, not as orphans
   are we left in sorrow now;
   Alleluia, he is near us,
   faith believes, nor questions how:
   though the cloud from sight received him,
   when the forty days were o'er,
   shall our hearts forget his promise,
   'I am with you evermore'?

3. Alleluia, bread of angels,
   thou on earth our food, our stay;
   Alleluia, here the sinful
   flee to thee from day to day:
   intercessor, friend of sinners,
   earth's redeemer, plead for me,
   where the songs of all the sinless
   sweep across the crystal sea.

4. Alleluia, King eternal,
   thee the Lord of lords we own;
   Alleluia, born of Mary,
   earth thy footstool, heaven thy throne:
   thou within the veil hast entered,
   robed in flesh, our great High Priest;
   thou on earth both priest and victim
   in the eucharistic feast.

HYFRYDOL 8 7. 8 7. D.
Text: William Chatterton Dix (1837-1898) Music: Richard Huw Pritchard (1811-1887)

11 Amazing grace

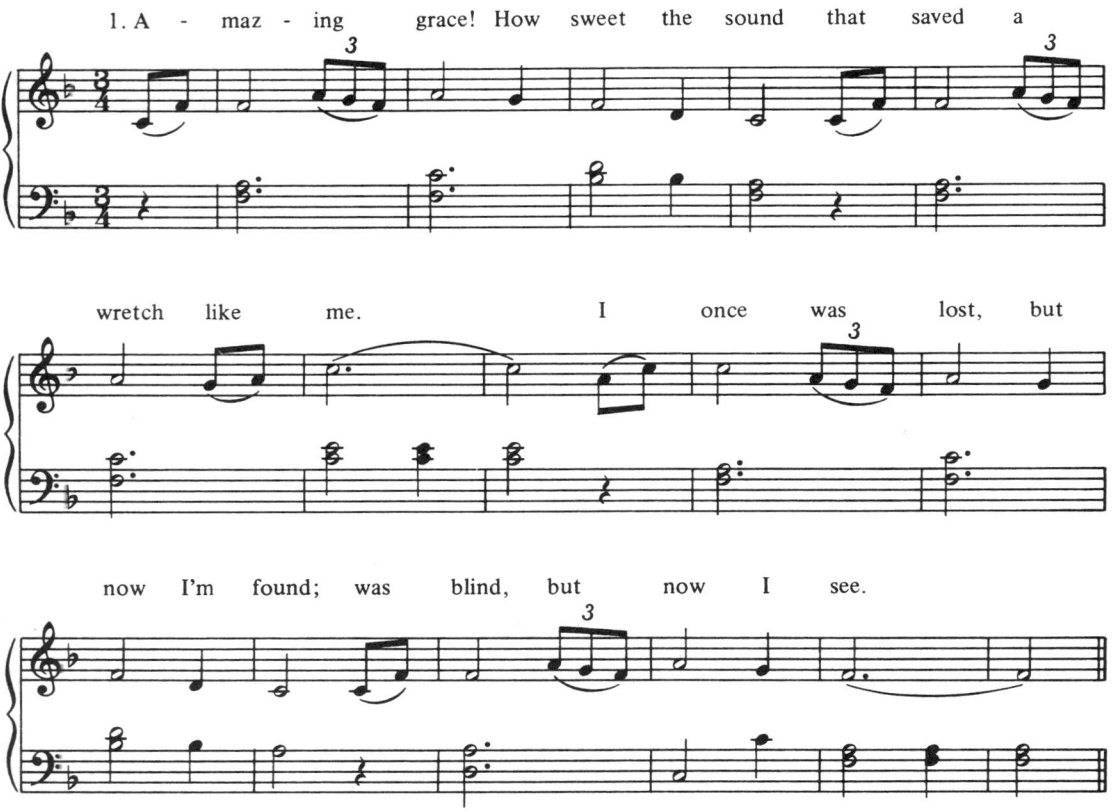

1. A-maz-ing grace! How sweet the sound that saved a wretch like me. I once was lost, but now I'm found; was blind, but now I see.

2. 'Twas grace that taught my heart to fear,
and grace my fears relieved.
How precious did that grace appear
the hour I first believed.

3. Through many dangers, toils and snares
I have already come.
'Tis grace hath brought me safe thus far,
and grace will lead me home.

4. The Lord has promised good to me;
his word my hope secured.
He will my shield and portion be
as long as life endures.

AMAZING GRACE C. M.
Text: John Newton (1725-1807)
Music: American Folk Melody

12 As with gladness

1. As with glad-ness men of old did the guid-ing star be-hold,
as with joy they hailed its light, lead-ing on-ward, beam-ing bright;
so, most gra-cious Lord, may we ev-er-more be led to thee.

2. As with joyful steps they sped,
Saviour, to thy lowly bed,
there to bend the knee before
thee whom heaven and earth adore;
so may we with willing feet
ever seek thy mercy-seat.

3. As they offered gifts most rare
at thy cradle rude and bare,
so may we with holy joy,
pure and free from sin's alloy,
all our costliest treasures bring,
Christ, to thee our heavenly King.

4. Holy Jesus, every day
keep us in the narrow way,
and, when earthly things are past,
bring our ransomed souls at last
where they need no star to guide,
where no clouds thy glory hide.

5. In the heavenly country bright
need they no created light;
thou its light, its joy, its crown,
thou its sun which goes not down;
there for ever may we sing
alleluias to our King.

DIX 77.77.77.
Text: William Chatterton Dix (1837-1898)
Music: Conrad Kocher (1786-1872), adapted by William Henry Monk (1823-1889)

13 At the name of Jesus

2. At his voice creation sprang at once to sight,
all the angel faces, all the hosts of light,
thrones and dominations, stars upon their way,
all the heavenly orders, in their great array.

3. Humbled for a season, to receive a name
from the lips of sinners unto whom he came,
faithfully he bore it spotless to the last,
brought it back victorious, when from death he passed.

4. Bore it up triumphant with its human light,
through all ranks of creatures, to the central height,
to the throne of Godhead, to the Father's breast;
filled it with the glory of that perfect rest.

5. Name him, brothers, name him, with love strong as death,
but with awe and wonder and with bated breath:
he is God the Saviour, he is Christ the Lord,
ever to be worshipped, trusted, and adored.

6. In your hearts enthrone him; there let him subdue
all that is not holy, all that is not true:
crown him as your captain in temptation's hour;
let his will enfold you in its light and power.

7. Brothers, this Lord Jesus shall return again,
with his Father's glory, with his angel train;
for all wreaths of empire meet upon his brow,
and our hearts confess him King of Glory now.

EVELYNS 6 5. 6 5. D.
Text: Caroline Maria Noel (1817-1877)   Music: William Henry Monk (1823-1889)

14 Be still and know

1. Be still and know that I am God, be still and know that I am God, be still and know that I am God.

2. I am the Lord that healeth thee. (*3 times*)

3. In thee, O Lord, I put my trust. (*3 times*)

BE STILL AND KNOW 8. 8. 8.
Text: v.1 Ps 46:10; v.2 Ex 15:26; v.3 Ps 141:8
Music: Unknown

15 Be thou my vision

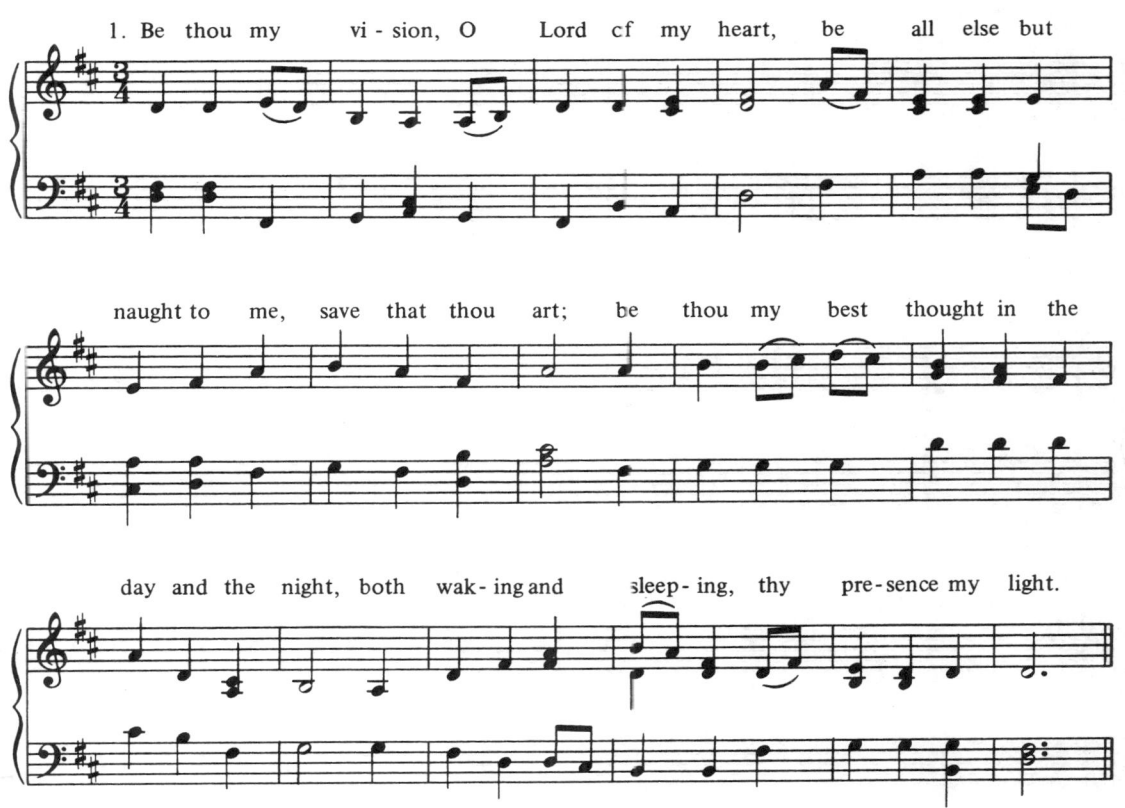

1. Be thou my vision, O Lord of my heart, be all else but naught to me, save that thou art; be thou my best thought in the day and the night, both waking and sleeping, thy presence my light.

2. Be thou my wisdom, be thou my true word,
   be thou ever with me, and I with thee, Lord;
   be thou my great Father, and I thy true son;
   be thou in me dwelling, and I with thee one.

3. Be thou my breastplate, my sword for the fight;
   be thou my whole armour, be thou my true might;
   be thou my soul's shelter, be thou my strong tower:
   O raise thou me heavenward, great power of my power.

4. Riches I heed not, nor man's empty praise:
   be thou mine inheritance now and always;
   be thou and thou only the first in my heart;
   O Sovereign of heaven, my treasure thou art.

5. High King of heaven, thou heaven's bright Sun,
   O grant me its joys after vict'ry is won;
   great heart of my own heart, whatever befall,
   still be thou my vision, O ruler of all.

SLANE 10 11. 11 11.
Text: Irish (8c.), translated by Mary Byrne (1880-1931), versified by Eleanor Hull (1860-1935)
Music: Traditional Irish Melody

16 Bind us together

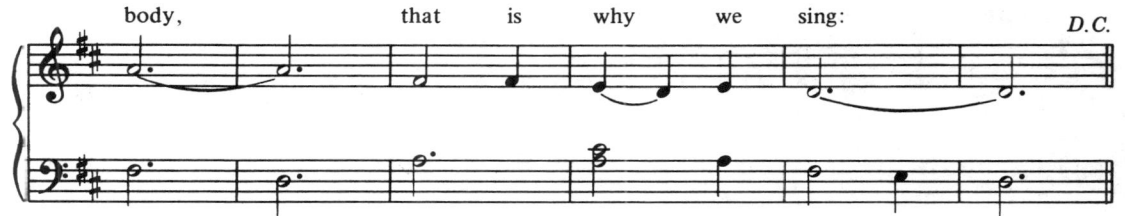

2. Made for the glory of God,
   purchased by his precious son.
   Born with the right to be clean,
   for Jesus the victory has won.

3. You are the family of God,
   you are the promise divine,
   you are God's chosen desire,
   you are the glorious new wine.

Text and Music: B. Gillman

17 Breathe on me, breath of God

1. Breathe on me, breath of God, fill me with life a-new, that
I may love what thou dost love, and do what thou wouldst do.

2. Breathe on me, breath of God,
   until my heart is pure:
   until with thee I have one will
   to do and to endure.

3. Breathe on me, breath of God,
   till I am wholly thine,
   until this earthly part of me
   glows with thy fire divine.

4. Breathe on me, breath of God,
   so shall I never die,
   but live with thee the perfect life
   of thine eternity.

CARLISLE S. M.
Text: Edwin Hatch (1835-1889) Music: Charles Lockhart (1745-1815)

18 Bright the vision that delighted

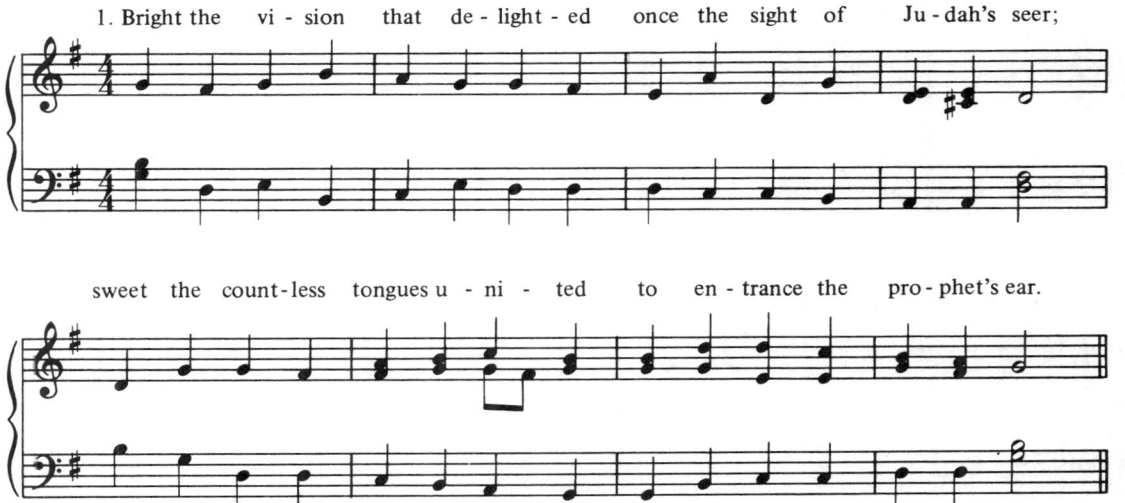

1. Bright the vi-sion that de-light-ed once the sight of Ju-dah's seer;

sweet the count-less tongues u-ni-ted to en-trance the pro-phet's ear.

2. Round the Lord in glory seated
   cherubim and seraphim
   filled his temple, and repeated
   each to each the alternate hymn:

3. 'Lord, thy glory fills the heaven;
   earth is with its fulness stored;
   unto thee be glory given,
   holy, holy, holy, Lord.'

4. Heaven is still with glory ringing,
   earth takes up the angels' cry,
   'Holy, holy, holy,' singing,
   'Lord of hosts, the Lord most high.'

5. With his seraph train before him,
   with his holy Church below,
   thus unite we to adore him,
   bid we thus our anthem flow:

6. 'Lord, thy glory fills the heaven;
   earth is with its fulness stored;
   unto thee be glory given,
   holy, holy, holy, Lord.'

LAUS DEO (REDHEAD NO. 46) 8 7. 8 7.
Text: Richard Mant (1776-1848)   Music: Richard Redhead (1820-1901)

19 Christ, whose glory fills the skies

1. Christ, whose glo - ry fills the skies, Christ, the true, the on - ly light,

sun of right - eous - ness, a - rise, tri - umph o'er the shades of night;

day - spring from on high, be near; day-spring, in my heart ap - pear.

2. Dark and cheerless is the morn
   unaccompanied by thee;
   joyless is the day's return,
   till thy mercy's beams I see,
   till they inward light impart,
   glad my eyes, and warm my heart.

3. Visit then this soul of mine,
   pierce the gloom of sin and grief;
   fill me, radiancy divine,
   scatter all my unbelief;
   more and more thyself display,
   shining to the perfect day.

RATISBON 7 7. 7 7. 7 7.
Text: Charles Wesley (1707-1788)
Music: Melody from Johann Gottlob Werner's *Choralbuch* (1815)

20 City of God

1. Ci - ty of God, how broad and far out - spread thy walls sub - lime; the true thy char - tered free - men are, of eve - ry age and clime.

2. One holy Church, one army strong,
   one steadfast, high intent;
   one working band, one harvest-song,
   one King omnipotent.

3. How purely hath thy speech come down
   from man's primaeval youth!
   How grandly hath thine empire grown
   of freedom, love, and truth!

4. How gleam thy watch-fires through the night
   with never-fainting ray!
   How rise thy towers, serene and bright,
   to meet the dawning day!

5. In vain the surge's angry shock,
   in vain the drifting sands:
   unharmed upon the eternal rock
   the eternal city stands.

RICHMOND C. M.
Text: Samuel Johnson (1822-1882) Music: Thomas Haweis (1734-1820)

21 Colours of day

Verse
1. Col - ours of day dawn in - to the mind, the sun has come up, the night is be - hind. Go down in the ci - ty, in - to the street, and let's give the mes-sage to the peo - ple we meet.

Chorus
So light up the fire and let the flame burn, o - pen the door, let Je - sus re - turn. Take

seeds of his Spi - rit, let the fruit grow, tell the

peo - ple of Je - sus, let his love show.

2. Go through the park, on into the town;
   the sun still shines on; it never goes down.
   The light of the world is risen again;
   the people of darkness are needing our friend.

3. Open your eyes, look into the sky,
   the darkness has come, the sun came to die.
   The evening draws on, the sun disappears,
   but Jesus is living, and his Spirit is near.

Words and Music: Sue McClellan, John Paculabo and Keith Rycroft

22 Come, thou Holy Spirit

1. Come, thou Ho - ly Spi - rit, come, and from thy ce - les - tial home

shed a ray of light di - vine; come, thou Fa - ther of the poor,

come, thou source of all our store, come, with - in our bos - oms shine:

2. Thou of comforters the best,
thou the soul's most welcome guest,
sweet refreshment here below;
in our labour rest most sweet,
grateful coolness in the heat,
solace in the midst of woe.

3. O most blessèd Light divine,
shine within these hearts of thine,
and our inmost being fill;
where thou art not, man hath naught,
nothing good in deed or thought,
nothing free from taint of ill.

4. Heal our wounds; our strength renew;
on our dryness pour thy dew;
wash the stains of guilt away;
bend the stubborn heart and will;
melt the frozen, warm the chill;
guide the steps that go astray.

5. On the faithful, who adore
and confess thee, evermore
in thy sevenfold gifts descend:
give them virtue's sure reward,
give them thy salvation, Lord,
give them joys that never end.

VENI SANCTE SPIRITUS 7 7 7. D.
Text: Stephen Langton (*d.*1228), translated by Edward Caswall (1814-1878)
Music: Samuel Webbe (1740-1816)

23 Come, thou long-expected Jesus

1. Come, thou long ex - pect - ed Je - sus, born to set thy peo - ple free, from our fears and sins re - lease us, let us find our rest in thee.

2. Israel's strength and consolation,
hope of all the earth thou art,
dear desire of every nation,
joy of every longing heart.

3. Born thy people to deliver,
born a child and yet a king,
born to reign in us for ever,
now thy gracious kingdom bring.

4. By thine own eternal Spirit,
rule in all our hearts alone;
by thine all-sufficient merit
raise us to thy glorious throne.

CROSS OF JESUS 8 7. 8 7.
Text: Charles Wesley (1707-1788) Music: John Stainer (1840-1901)

24 Come, ye thankful people

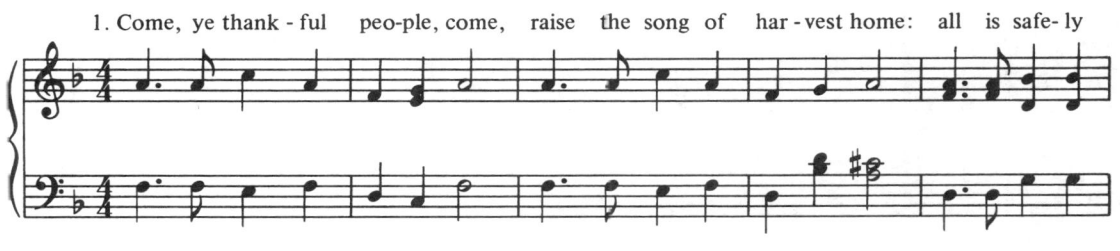

1. Come, ye thank-ful peo-ple, come, raise the song of har-vest home: all is safe-ly

ga - thered in, ere the win-ter storms be - gin; God, our ma-ker, doth pro-vide

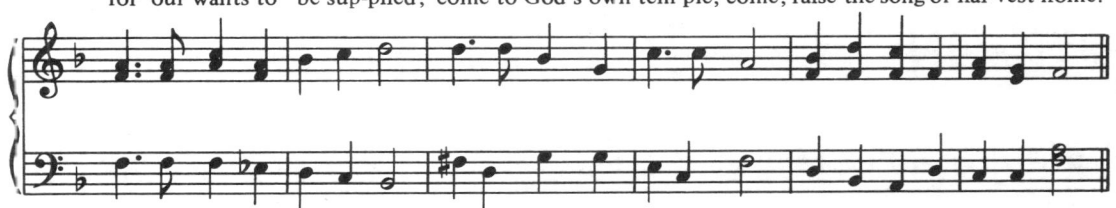

for our wants to be sup-plied; come to God's own tem-ple, come; raise the song of har-vest home.

2. All this world is God's own field,
   fruit unto his praise to yield;
   wheat and tares therein are sown,
   unto joy or sorrow grown;
   ripening with a wondrous power
   till the final harvest-hour:
   grant, O Lord of life, that we
   holy grain and pure may be.

3. For we know that thou wilt come,
   and wilt take thy people home;
   from the field wilt purge away
   all that doth offend, that day;
   and thine angels charge at last
   in the fire the tares to cast,
   but the fruitful ears to store
   in thy garner evermore.

4. Come then, Lord of mercy, come,
   bid us sing thy harvest-home:
   let thy saints be gathered in,
   free from sorrow, free from sin:
   all upon the golden floor
   praising thee for evermore:
   come, with all thine angels come,
   bid us sing thy harvest-home.

ST GEORGE 7 7. 7 7. D.
Text: Henry Alford (1810-1871) Music: George Job Elvey (1816-1893)

25 Crown him with many crowns

2. Crown him the virgin's son,
   the God incarnate born,
   whose arm those crimson trophies won
   which now his brow adorn:
   fruit of the mystic rose,
   as of that rose the stem;
   the root whence mercy ever flows,
   the babe of Bethlehem.

3. Crown him the Lord of love;
   behold his hands and side,
   those wounds yet visible above
   in beauty glorified:
   no angel in the sky
   can fully bear that sight,
   but downward bends his burning eye
   at mysteries so bright.

4. Crown him the Lord of peace
   whose power a sceptre sways
   from pole to pole, that wars may cease,
   and all be prayer and praise:
   his reign shall know no end,
   and round his piercèd feet
   fair flowers of paradise extend
   their fragrance ever sweet.

5. Crown him the Lord of years,
   the potentate of time,
   creator of the rolling spheres,
   ineffably sublime:
   all hail, Redeemer, hail!
   for thou hast died for me;
   thy praise shall never, never fail
   throughout eternity.

DIADEMATA D. S. M.
Text: Matthew Bridges (1800-1894) Music: George Job Elvey (1816-1893)

26 Dear Lord and Father of mankind

2. In simple trust like theirs who heard,
   beside the Syrian sea,
   the gracious calling of the Lord,
   let us, like them, without a word
   rise up and follow thee.

3. O Sabbath rest by Galilee!
   O calm of hills above,
   where Jesus knelt to share with thee
   the silence of eternity,
   interpreted by love!

4. Drop thy still dews of quietness,
   till all our strivings cease;
   take from our souls the strain and stress,
   and let our ordered lives confess
   the beauty of thy peace.

5. Breathe through the heats of our desire
   thy coolness and thy balm;
   let sense be dumb, let flesh retire;
   speak through the earthquake, wind, and fire,
   O still small voice of calm.

REPTON 8 6. 8 8 6.
Text: John Greenleaf Whittier (1807-1892)   Music: Charles Hubert Hastings Parry (1848-1918)

27 Earth has many a noble city

2. Fairer than the sun at morning
   was the star that told his birth,
   to the world its God announcing
   seen in fleshly form on earth.

3. Eastern sages at his cradle
   make oblations rich and rare;
   see them give in deep devotion
   gold and frankincense and myrrh.

4. Sacred gifts of mystic meaning:
   incense doth their God disclose,
   gold the King of kings proclaimeth,
   myrrh his sepulchre foreshows.

5. Jesu, whom the Gentiles worshipped
   at thy glad Epiphany,
   unto thee with God the Father
   and the Spirit glory be.

STUTTGART 8 7. 8 7.
Text: Prudentius (348-*c.* 413), translated by Edward Caswall (1814-1878)
Music: Christian Friedrich Witt (1660-1716)

28 Eternal Father, strong to save

1. E - ter - nal Fa - ther, strong to save, whose arm hath bound the rest - less wave, who bidd'st the migh - ty o - cean deep its own ap - poin - ted li - mits keep: O hear us when we cry to thee for those in pe - ril on the sea.

2. O Christ, whose voice the waters heard
and hushed their raging at thy word,
who walkedst on the foaming deep,
and calm amid the storm didst sleep:
O hear us when we cry to thee
for those in peril on the sea.

3. O Holy Spirit, who didst brood
upon the waters dark and rude,
and bid their angry tumult cease,
and give, for wild confusion, peace:
O hear us when we cry to thee
for those in peril on the sea.

4. O Trinity of love and power,
our brethren shield in danger's hour;
from rock and tempest, fire and foe,
protect them wheresoe'er they go:
thus evermore shall rise to thee
glad hymns of praise from land and sea.

MELITA 8 8. 8 8. 8 8.
Text: William Whiting (1825-1878) Music: John Bacchus Dykes (1823-1876)

29 Fight the good fight

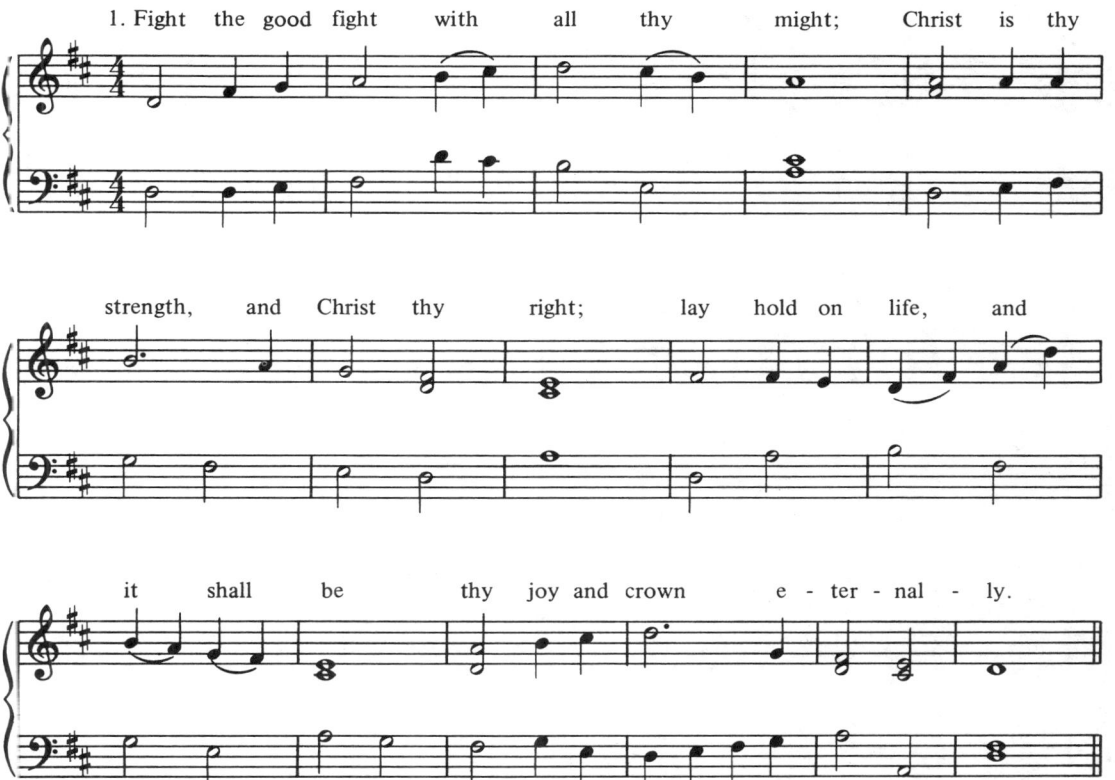

1. Fight the good fight with all thy might; Christ is thy strength, and Christ thy right; lay hold on life, and it shall be thy joy and crown e-ter-nal-ly.

2. Run the straight race through God's good grace,
   lift up thine eyes, and seek his face;
   life with its way before us lies;
   Christ is the path, and Christ the prize.

3. Cast care aside, lean on thy guide;
   his boundless mercy will provide;
   trust, and thy trusting soul shall prove
   Christ is its life, and Christ its love.

4. Faint not nor fear, his arms are near;
   he changeth not, and thou art dear;
   only believe, and thou shalt see
   that Christ is all in all to thee.

DUKE STREET L. M.
Text: John Samuel Bewley Monsell (1811-1875)   Music: Attributed to John Hatton (*d.*1793)

30 For I'm building a people of power

Text and Music: Dave Richards

31 Forty days and forty nights

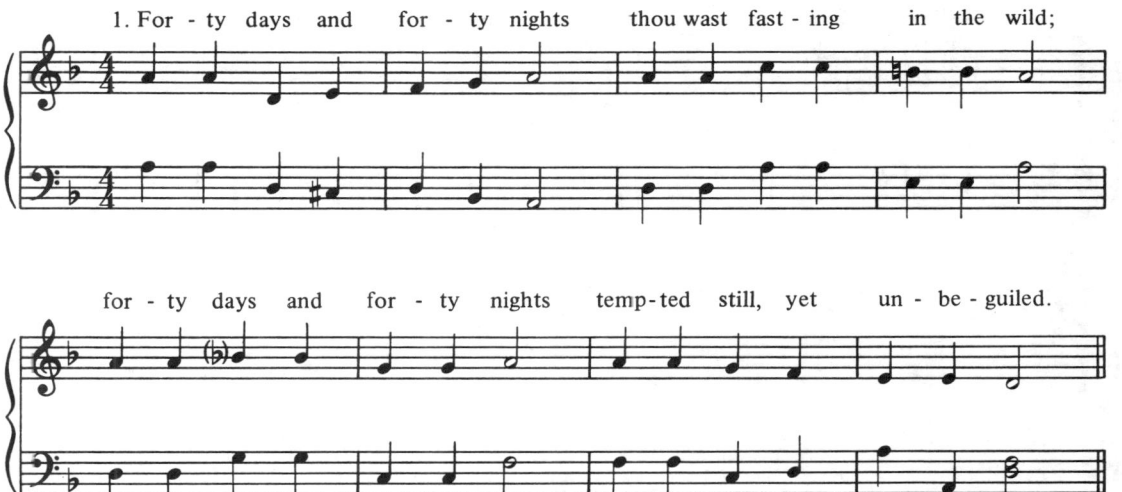

2. Sunbeams scorching all the day,
chilly dew-drops nightly shed,
prowling beasts about thy way,
stones thy pillow, earth thy bed.

3. Let us thy endurance share
and from earthly greed abstain,
with thee watching unto prayer,
with thee strong to suffer pain.

4. Then if evil on us press,
flesh or spirit to assail,
victor in the wilderness,
help us not to swerve or fail!

5. So shall peace divine be ours;
holier gladness ours shall be,
come to us angelic powers,
such as ministered to thee.

6. Keep, O keep us, Saviour dear,
ever constant by thy side,
that with thee we may appear
at the eternal Eastertide.

AUS DER TIEFE 7 7. 7 7.
Text: George Hunt Smyttan (1822-1870) and others
Music: Melody from *Nürnbergisches Gesangbuch* (1676)

32 Give me joy in my heart

Verse

1. Give me joy in my heart, keep me prais-ing, give me joy in my heart I pray. Give me

joy in my heart, keep me prais-ing keep me prais-ing till the break of day.

Chorus

Sing ho-san-na! Sing ho-san-na! Sing ho-san-na to the King of kings!

Sing ho-san-na! Sing ho-san-na! Sing ho-san-na to the King!

2. Give me peace in my heart, keep me resting,
   give me peace in my heart, I pray.
   Give me peace in my heart, keep me resting.
   Keep me resting till the end of the day.

3. Give me love in my heart, keep me serving,
   give me love in my heart, I pray.
   Give me love in my heart, keep me serving,
   keep me serving till the end of day.

SING HOSANNA 10 8. 10 9.
Text and Music: Traditional

33 Glory to thee, my God

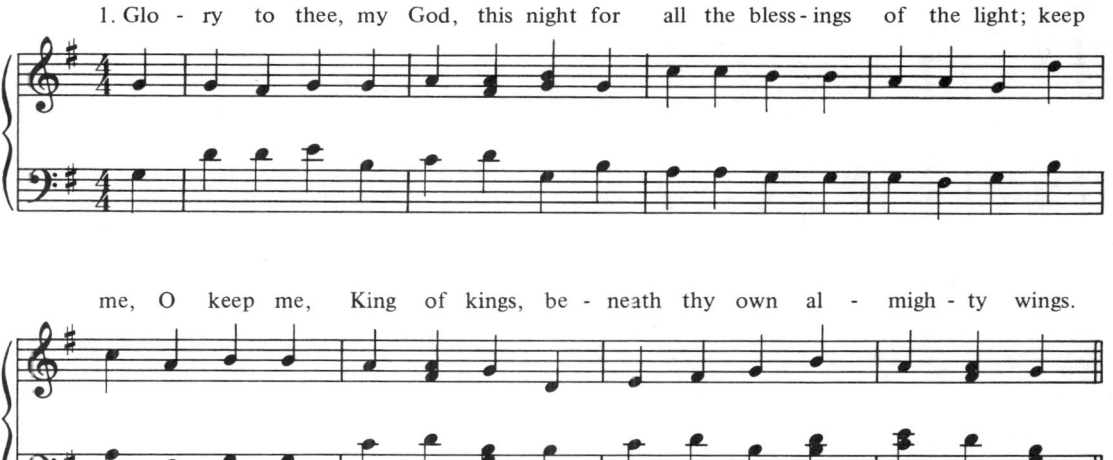

1. Glo-ry to thee, my God, this night for all the bless-ings of the light; keep me, O keep me, King of kings, be-neath thy own al-migh-ty wings.

2. Forgive me, Lord, for thy dear Son,
the ill that I this day have done,
that with the world, myself, and thee,
I, ere I sleep, at peace may be.

3. Teach me to live, that I may dread
the grave as little as my bed;
teach me to die, that so I may
rise glorious at the awful day.

4. O may my soul on thee repose,
and may sweet sleep mine eyelids close,
sleep that may me more vigorous make
to serve my God when I awake.

5. When in the night I sleepless lie,
my soul with heavenly thoughts supply;
let no ill dreams disturb my rest,
no powers of darkness me molest.

6. Praise God, from whom all blessings flow,
praise him, all creatures here below,
praise him above, angelic host,
praise Father, Son, and Holy Ghost.

TALLIS'S CANON L. M.
Text: Thomas Ken (1637-1711) Music: Thomas Tallis (c.1505-1585)

34 God forgave my sin *(Freely, freely)*

Verse

1. God for - gave my sin in Je - sus' name. I've been born a -
gain in Je - sus' name. And in Je - sus' name I
come to you to share his love as he told me to.
He said: 'Free - ly, free - ly you have re - ceived;
free - ly, free - ly give.

Go in my name, and be - cause you be - lieve,

oth - ers will know that I live.'

2. All pow'r is giv'n in Jesus' name,
   in earth and heav'n in Jesus' name.
   And in Jesus' name I come to you
   to share his pow'r as he told me to.

3. God gives us life in Jesus' name,
   he lives in us in Jesus' name.
   And in Jesus' name I come to you
   to share his peace as he told me to.

Text and Music: Carol Owens

35 God is love

Verse

1. God is love; his the care, tend-ing each, eve-ry-where. God is love, all is there! Je-sus came to show him, that man-kind might know him!

Chorus

Sing a-loud, loud, loud! Sing a-loud, loud, loud! God is good! God is truth! God is beau-ty! Praise him!

2. None can see God above;
   all have here man to love;
   thus may we Godward move,
   finding him in others,
   holding all men brothers.

3. Jesus lived here for men:
   strove and died, rose again,
   rules our hearts, now as then;
   for he came to save us
   by the truth he gave us.

4. To our Lord praise we sing,
   light and life, friend and King,
   coming down love to bring,
   pattern for our duty,
   showing God in beauty.

PERSONENT HODIE (THEODORIC) 6 6. 6 6 6.
Text: Percy Dearmer (1867-1936)   Music: Melody from *Piae Cantiones* (1582)

36 Guide me, O thou great Redeemer

1. Guide me, O thou great Redeemer, pilgrim through this barren land; I am weak, but thou art mighty; hold me with thy powerful hand; bread of heaven, bread of heaven, feed me till I want no more, feed me till I want no more.

2. Open now the crystal fountain,
   whence the healing stream doth flow;
   let the fire and cloudy pillar
   lead me all my journey through;
   strong deliverer, strong deliverer,
   by thou still my strength and shield.

3. When I tread the verge of Jordan,
   bid my anxious fears subside,
   death of death, and hell's destruction,
   land me safe on Canaan's side;
   songs of praises, songs of praises,
   I will ever give to thee.

CWM RHONDDA 8 7. 8 7. 4 4 7.
Text: William Williams (1717-1791), translated by Peter Williams (1727-1796) and others
Music: John Hughes (1873-1932)

37 Hail the day that sees him rise

2. There for him high triumph waits;
   lift your heads, eternal gates!
   he hath conquered death and sin;
   take the King of Glory in!

3. Lo, the heaven its Lord receives,
   yet he loves the earth he leaves;
   though returning to his throne,
   still he calls mankind his own.

4. See, he lifts his hands above;
   see, he shews the prints of love;
   hark, his gracious lips bestow
   blessings on his Church below.

5. Still for us he intercedes,
   his prevailing death he pleads;
   near himself prepares our place,
   he the first-fruits of our race.

6. Lord, though parted from our sight,
   far above the starry height,
   grant our hearts may thither rise,
   seeking thee above the skies.

LLANFAIR 7 7. 7 7.
Text: Charles Wesley (1707-1788), Thomas Cotterill (1779-1823) and others
Music: Robert Williams (1781-1821)

38 Hark, a thrilling voice is sounding

1. Hark, a thrill-ing voice is sound-ing: 'Christ is nigh,' it seems to say; cast a-way the dreams of dark-ness, O ye child-ren of the day.

2. Wakened by the solemn warning,
   let the earth-bound soul arise;
   Christ, her Sun, all ill dispelling,
   shines upon the morning skies.

3. Lo, the Lamb, so long expected,
   comes with pardon down from heaven;
   let us haste, with tears of sorrow,
   one and all to be forgiven;

4. That when next he comes with glory,
   and the world is wrapped in fear,
   with his mercy he may shield us,
   and with words of love draw near.

5. Honour, glory, might, and blessing
   to the Father and the Son,
   with the everlasting Spirit,
   while eternal ages run.

MERTON 8 7. 8 7.
Text: Translated from the Latin by Edward Caswall (1814-1878)
Music: William Henry Monk (1823-1889)

39 Hark the glad sound!

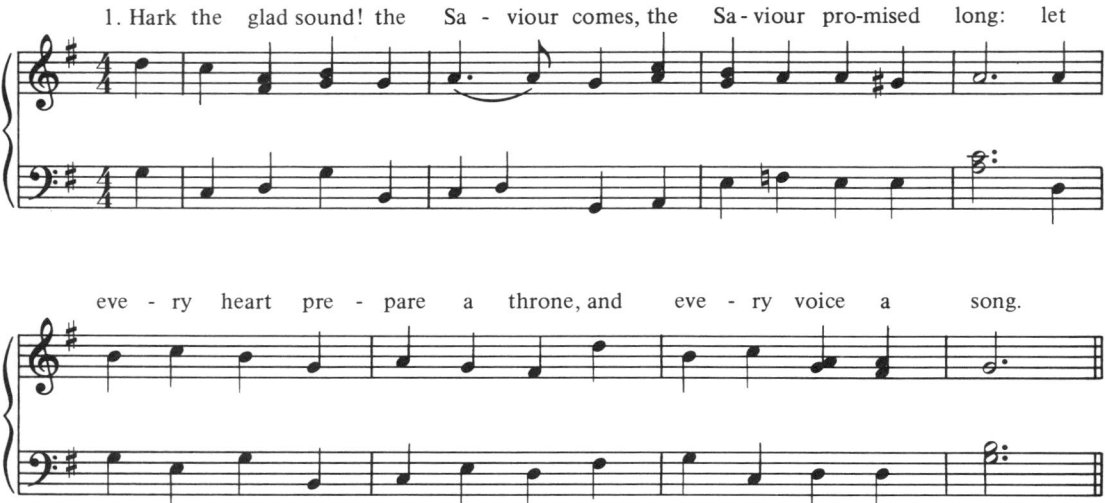

1. Hark the glad sound! the Sa-viour comes, the Sa-viour pro-mised long: let
eve-ry heart pre-pare a throne, and eve-ry voice a song.

2. He comes, the prisoners to release
in Satan's bondage held;
the gates of brass before him burst,
the iron fetters yield.

3. He comes, the broken heart to bind,
the bleeding soul to cure,
and with the treasures of his grace
to bless the humble poor.

4. Our glad hosannas, Prince of Peace,
thy welcome shall proclaim;
and heaven's eternal arches ring
with thy belovèd name.

BRISTOL C.M.
Text: Philip Doddridge (1702-1751)
Music: Melody from Thomas Ravenscroft's *Psalmes* (1621)

40 He is Lord

2. He is King, he is King.
   He is risen from the dead and he is King.
   Ev'ry knee shall bow, ev'ry tongue confess
   that Jesus Christ is King.

3. He is love, he is love.
   He is risen from the dead and he is love.
   Ev'ry knee shall bow, ev'ry tongue confess
   that Jesus Christ is love.

Text and Music: Unknown

41 He's got the whole world in his hand

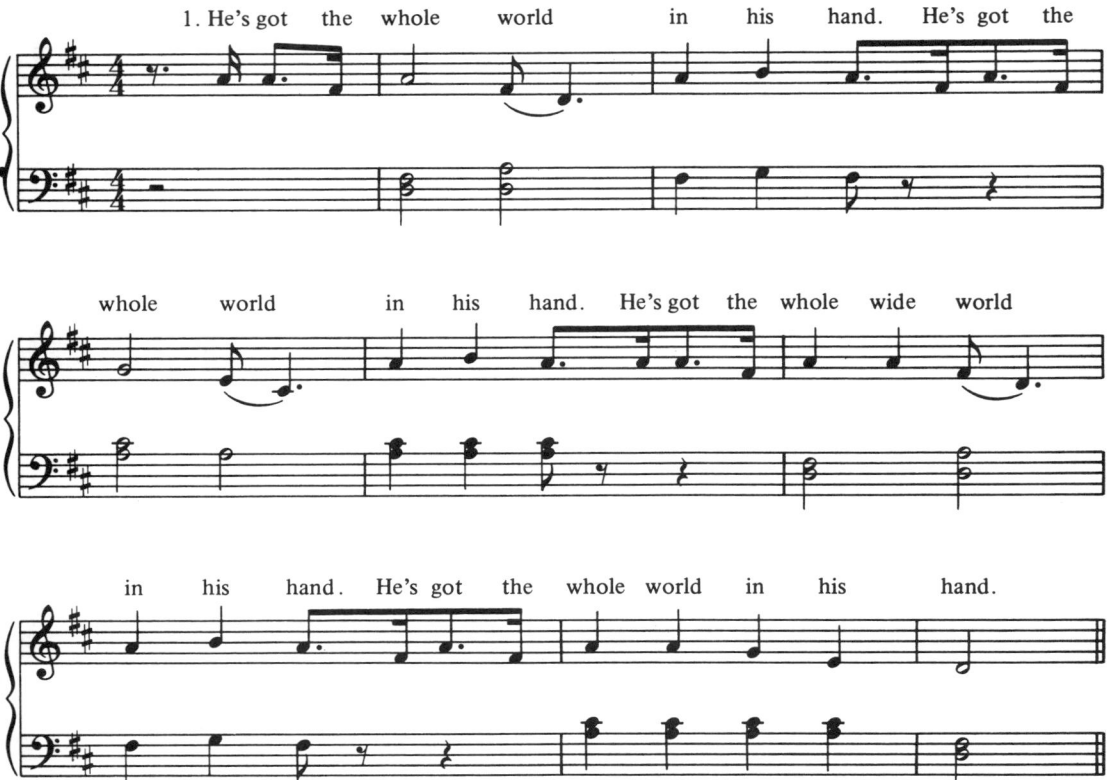

2. He's got you and me, brother in his hand. (3)
He's got the whole world in his hand.

3. He's got you and me, sister in his hand. (3)
He's got the whole world in his hand.

4. He's got the tiny little baby in his hand. (3)
He's got the whole world in his hand.

5. He's got everybody here in his hand. (3)
He's got the whole world in his hand.

Text and Music: Traditional

42 Holy, holy, holy!

2. Holy, holy, holy! All the saints adore thee,
   casting down their golden crowns around the glassy sea;
   cherubim and seraphim falling down before thee,
   which wert and art and evermore shalt be.

3. Holy, holy, holy! Though the darkness hide thee,
   though the eye of sinful man thy glory may not see,
   only thou art holy, there is none beside thee
   perfect in power, in love, and purity.

4. Holy, holy, holy! Lord God almighty!
   all thy works shall praise thy name in earth and sky and sea;
   holy, holy, holy! Merciful and mighty!
   God in three persons, blessed Trinity!

NICAEA 11 12. 12 10.
Text: Reginald Heber (1783-1826) John Bacchus Dykes (1823-1876)

43 How lovely on the mountains

2. You watchmen, lift your voices joyfully as one,
   shout for your King, your King!
   See eye to eye, the Lord restoring Sion:
   Our God reigns. (6)

3. Wasteplaces of Jerusalem, break forth with joy!
   We are redeemed, redeemed.
   The Lord has saved and comforted his people.
   Our God reigns. (6)

4. Ends of the earth, see the salvation of our God!
   Jesus is Lord, is Lord!
   Before the nations he has bared his holy arm.
   Our God reigns. (6)

Text and Music: Leonard E Smith Jr.

44 Immortal, invisible

2. Unresting, unhasting, and silent as light,
   nor wanting, nor wasting, thou rulest in might;
   thy justice like mountains high soaring above
   thy clouds which are fountains of goodness and love.

3. To all life thou givest, to both great and small;
   in all life thou livest, the true life of all;
   we blossom and flourish as leaves on the tree,
   and wither and perish; but naught changeth thee.

4. Great Father of glory, pure Father of light,
   thine angels adore thee, all veiling their sight;
   all laud we would render: O help us to see
   'tis only the splendour of light hideth thee.

ST DENIO 11 11. 11 11.
Text: Walter Chalmers Smith (1824-1908)
Music: Welsh Melody from John Robert's *Caniadau y Cyssegre* (1839)

45 Jesus Christ is risen today

2. Hymns of praise then let us sing, alleluia,
   unto Christ, our heavenly King, alleluia,
   who endured the cross and grave, alleluia,
   sinners to redeem and save, alleluia.

3. But the pains that he endured, alleluia,
   our salvation have procured, alleluia,
   now above the sky he's King, alleluia,
   where the angels ever sing, alleluia.

EASTER HYMN 7 7. 7 7.
Text: From *Lyra Davidica* (1708) and *The Supplement* (1816)
Music: Adapated from a Melody in *Lyra Davidica*, (1708)

46 Jesus shall reign where'er the sun

2. People and realms of every tongue
   dwell on his love with sweetest song,
   and infant voices shall proclaim
   their early blessings on his name.

3. Blessings abound where'er he reigns:
   the prisoner leaps to lose his chains;
   the weary find eternal rest,
   and all the sons of want are blest.

4. To him shall endless prayer be made,
   and praises throng to crown his head;
   his name like incense shall arise
   with every morning sacrifice.

5. Let every creature rise and bring
   peculiar honours to our King;
   angels descend with songs again,
   and earth repeat the loud Amen.

TRURO L. M.

Text: Isaac Watts (1674-1748) Music: Melody from Thomas Williams' *Psalmodia Evangelica* (1789)

47 Jesus, where'er thy people meet

1. Je - sus, wher - e'er thy peo - ple meet, there they be -
hold thy mer - cy seat; wher - e'er they seek thee
thou art found, and eve - ry place is hall - owed ground.

2. For thou, within no walls confined,
   inhabitest the humble mind;
   such ever bring thee when they come,
   and, going, take thee to their home.

3. Dear Shepherd of thy chosen few,
   thy former mercies here renew;
   here to our waiting hearts proclaim
   the sweetness of thy saving name.

4. Here may we prove the power of prayer
   to strengthen faith and sweeten care,
   to teach our faint desires to rise,
   and bring all heaven before our eyes.

5. Lord, we are few, but thou art near;
   nor short thine arm, nor deaf thine ear:
   O rend the heavens, come quickly down,
   and make a thousand hearts thine own.

WAREHAM L. M.
Text: William Cowper (1731-1800)   William Knapp (1698-1768)

48 Just as I am

1. Just as I am, with-out one plea but that thy
blood was shed for me, and that thou bidst me
come to thee, O Lamb of God, I come.

2. Just as I am, though tossed about
with many a conflict, many a doubt,
fightings and fears within, without,
O Lamb of God, I come.

3. Just as I am, poor, wretched, blind;
sight, riches, healing of the mind,
yea, all I need, in thee to find,
O Lamb of God, I come.

4. Just as I am, thou wilt receive,
wilt welcome, pardon, cleanse, relieve:
because thy promise I believe,
O Lamb of God, I come.

5. Just as I am (thy love unknown
has broken every barrier down),
now to be thine, yea, thine alone,
O Lamb of God, I come.

6. Just as I am, of that free love
the breadth, length, depth, and height to prove,
here for a season, then above,
O Lamb of God, I come.

SAFFRON WALDEN 8 8 8. 6.
Text: Charlotte Elliott (1789-1871) Music: Arthur Henry Brown (1830-1926)

49 King of Glory, King of Peace

1. King of glo - ry, King of peace, I will love thee;

and, that love may ne - ver cease, I will move thee.

Thou hast grant - ed my re - quest, thou hast heard me;

thou didst note my work - ing breast, thou hast spared me.

2. Wherefore with my utmost art
   I will sing thee,
   and the cream of all my heart
   I will bring thee.
   Though my sins against me cried,
   thou didst clear me,
   and alone, when they replied,
   thou didst hear me.

3. Seven whole days, not one in seven,
   I will praise thee;
   in my heart, though not in heaven,
   I can raise thee.
   Small it is, in this poor sort
   to enrol thee:
   e'en eternity's too short
   to extol thee.

GWALCHMAI 7 4. 7 4. D.
Text: George Herbert (1593-1633) Music: Joseph David Jones (1827-1870)

50 Kum ba yah

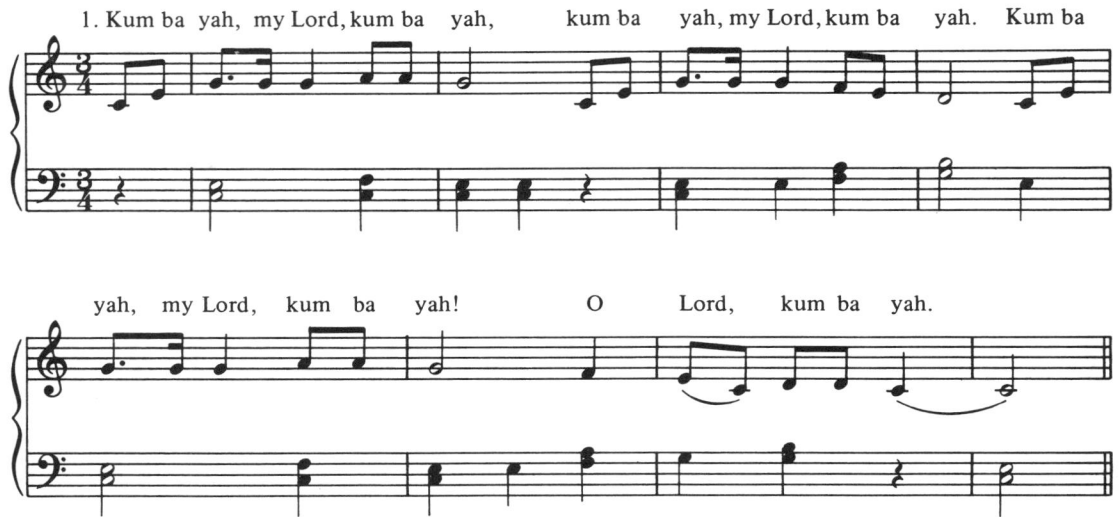

2. Someone's crying, Lord, kum ba yah. (3)
   O Lord, kum ba yah.

3. Someone's singing, Lord, kum ba yah. (3)
   O Lord, kum ba yah.

4. Someone's praying, Lord, kum ba yah. (3)
   O Lord, kum ba yah.

Text and Music: Spiritual

51 Lead us, heavenly Father

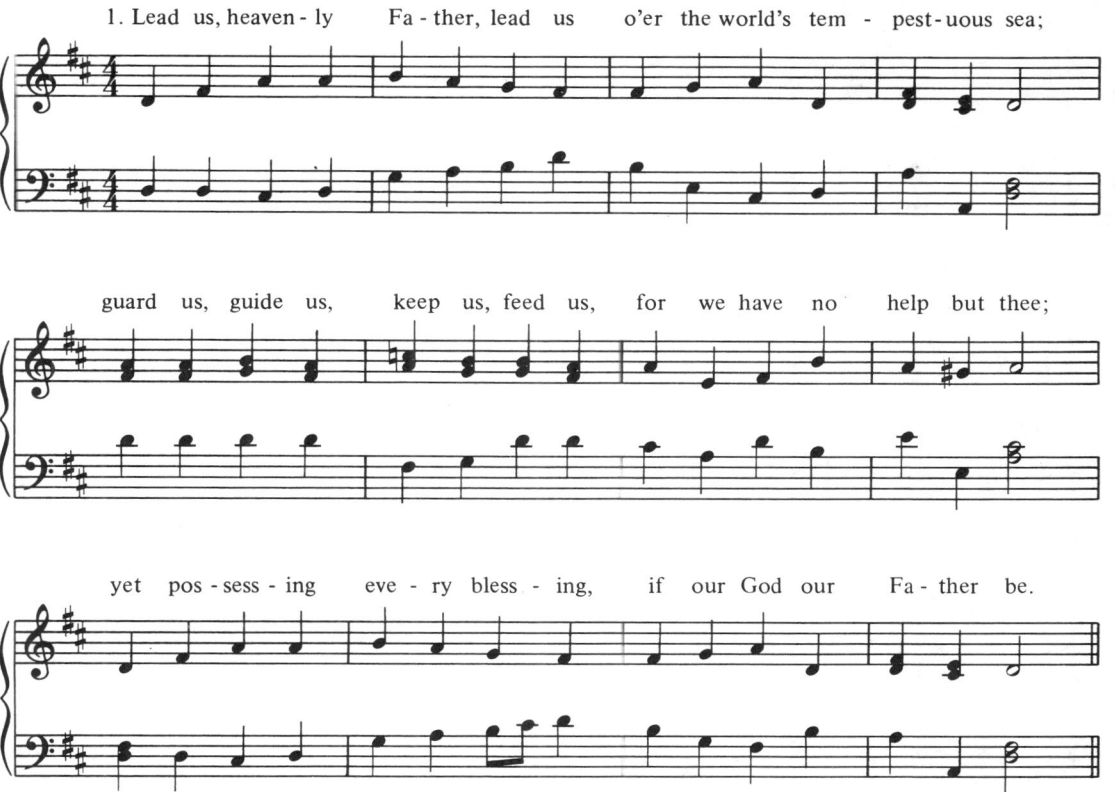

1. Lead us, heaven-ly Fa-ther, lead us o'er the world's tem-pest-uous sea;

guard us, guide us, keep us, feed us, for we have no help but thee;

yet pos-sess-ing eve-ry bless-ing, if our God our Fa-ther be.

2. Saviour, breathe forgiveness o'er us:
   all our weakness thou dost know;
   thou didst tread this earth before us,
   thou didst feel its keenest woe;
   lone and dreary, faint and weary,
   through the desert thou didst go.

3. Spirit of our God, descending,
   fill our hearts with heavenly joy,
   love with every passion blending,
   pleasure that can never cloy:
   thus provided, pardoned, guided,
   nothing can our peace destroy.

MANNHEIM 8 7. 8 7. 8 7.
Text: James Edmeston (1791-1867) Music: Friedrich Filitz (1804-1876)

52 Let all mortal flesh

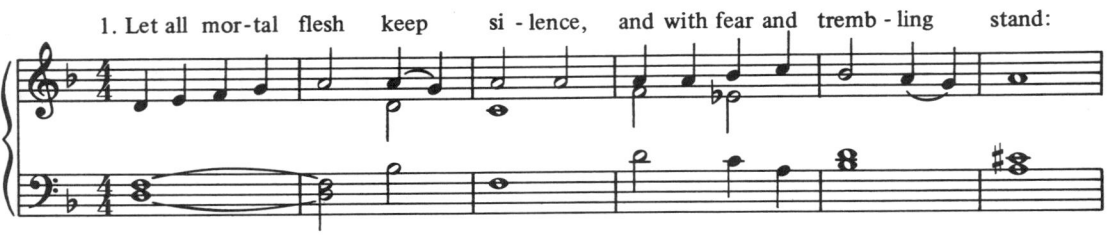

1. Let all mor-tal flesh keep si-lence, and with fear and tremb-ling stand:

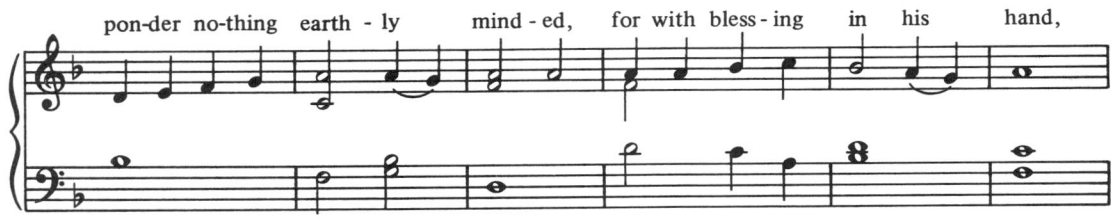

pon-der no-thing earth-ly mind-ed, for with bless-ing in his hand,

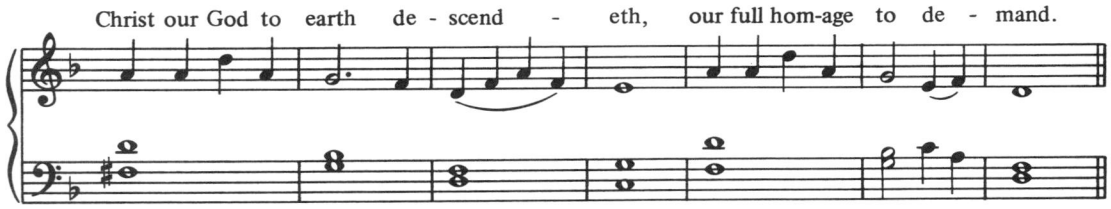

Christ our God to earth de-scend - eth, our full hom-age to de - mand.

2. King of kings, yet born of Mary,
as of old on earth he stood,
Lord of lords, in human vesture –
in the body and the blood –
he will give to all the faithful
his own self for heavenly food.

3. Rank on rank the host of heaven
spreads its vanguard on the way,
as the light of light descendeth
from the realms of endless day,
that the powers of hell may vanish
as the darkness clears away.

4. At his feet the six-winged seraph;
cherubim with sleepless eye
veil their faces to the presence,
as with ceaseless voice they cry,
alleluia, alleluia,
alleluia, Lord most high.

PICARDY 8 7. 8 7. 8 7.
Text: Liturgy of St James, translated by Gerard Moultrie (1829-1885)
Music: Traditional French Carol from Tiersot's *Mélodies*, Paris (1887)

53 Let all the world in every corner sing

2. Let all world in every corner sing,
   my God and King.
   The Church with psalms must shout,
   no door can keep them out;
   but above all the heart
   must bear the longest part.
   Let all the world in every corner sing,
   my God and King.

LUCKINGTON 10 4. 6 6. 6 6. 10 4.
Text: George Herbert (1593-1633) Music: Basil Harwood (1859-1949)

54 Let us with a gladsome mind

1. Let us with a glad-some mind, praise the Lord, for he is kind:

for his mer-cies aye en-dure, ev - er faith-ful, ev - er sure.

2. Let us blaze his name abroad,
   for of gods he is the God:
   for his mercies aye endure,
   ever faithful, ever sure.

3. He with all-commanding might
   filled the new-made world with light:
   for his mercies aye endure,
   ever faithful, ever sure.

4. He the golden-tressèd sun
   caused all day his course to run:
   for his mercies aye endure,
   ever faithful, ever sure.

5. And the hornèd moon at night
   'mid her spangled sisters bright:
   for his mercies aye endure
   ever faithful, ever sure.

6. All things living he doth feed,
   his full hand supplies their need:
   for his mercies aye endure,
   ever faithful, ever sure.

7. Let us, with a gladsome mind,
   praise the Lord, for he is kind:
   for his mercies aye endure,
   ever faithful, ever sure.

MONKLAND 7 7. 7 7.
Text: John Milton (1608-1674)   Music: John Antes (1740-1811)

55 Light's abode, celestial Salem

1. Light's a-bode, ce-les-tial Sa-lem, vi-sion whence true peace doth spring,

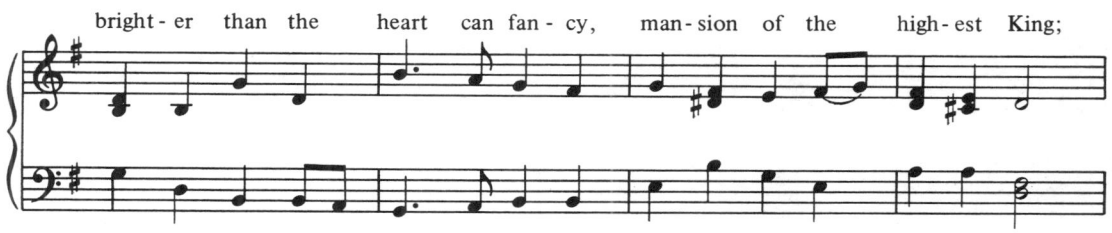

bright-er than the heart can fan-cy, man-sion of the high-est King;

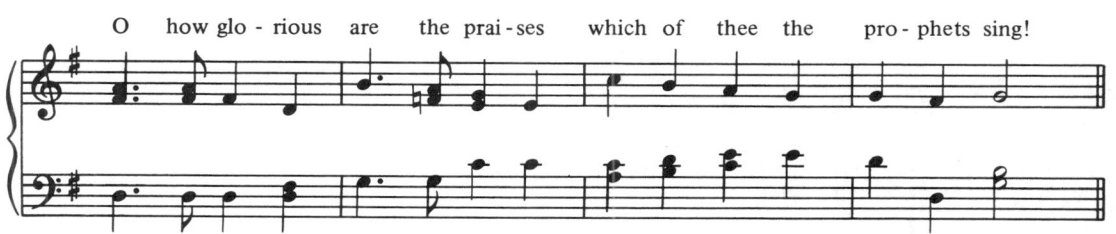

O how glo-rious are the prai-ses which of thee the pro-phets sing!

2. There for ever and for ever
   alleluia is outpoured;
   for unending, for unbroken
   is the feast-day of the Lord;
   all is pure and all is holy
   that within thy walls is stored.

3. There no cloud or passing vapour
   dims the brightness of the air;
   endless noon-day, glorious noon-day,
   from the Sun of suns is there;
   there no night brings rest from labour,
   for unknown are toil and care.

4. O how glorious and resplendent,
   fragile body, shalt thou be,
   when endued with so much beauty,
   full of health and strong and free,
   full of vigour, full of pleasure
   that shall last eternally.

5. Now with gladness, now with courage,
   bear the burden on thee laid,
   that hereafter these thy labours
   may with endless gifts be paid;
   and in everlasting glory
   thou with brightness be arrayed.

6. Laud and honour to the Father,
   laud and honour to the Son,
   laud and honour to the Spirit,
   ever three and ever one,
   consubstantial, co-eternal,
   while unending ages run.

REGENT SQUARE 8 7. 8 7. 8 7.
Text: Ascribed to Thomas à Kempis (c.1380-1471), translated by John Mason Neale (1818-1866)
Music: Henry Smart (1813-1879)

56 Lo, he comes with clouds descending

Al - le-lu - ia! Christ ap - pears on earth to reign.

2. Every eye shall now behold him
   robed in dreadful majesty;
   those who set at naught and sold him,
   pierced and nailed him to the tree,
   deeply wailing, (3)
   shall the true Messiah see.

3. Those dear tokens of his passion
   still his dazzling body bears,
   cause of endless exultation
   to his ransomed worshippers:
   with what rapture (3)
   gaze we on those glorious scars!

4. Yea, Amen, let all adore thee,
   high on thine eternal throne;
   Saviour, take the power and glory,
   claim the kingdom for thine own;
   Alleluia! (3)
   thou shalt reign, and thou alone.

HELMSLEY 8 7. 8 7. 8 7.
Text: Charles Wesley (1707-1788) and John Cennick (1718-1755)
Music: From John Wesley's *Select Hymns* (1765)

57 Lo, round the throne

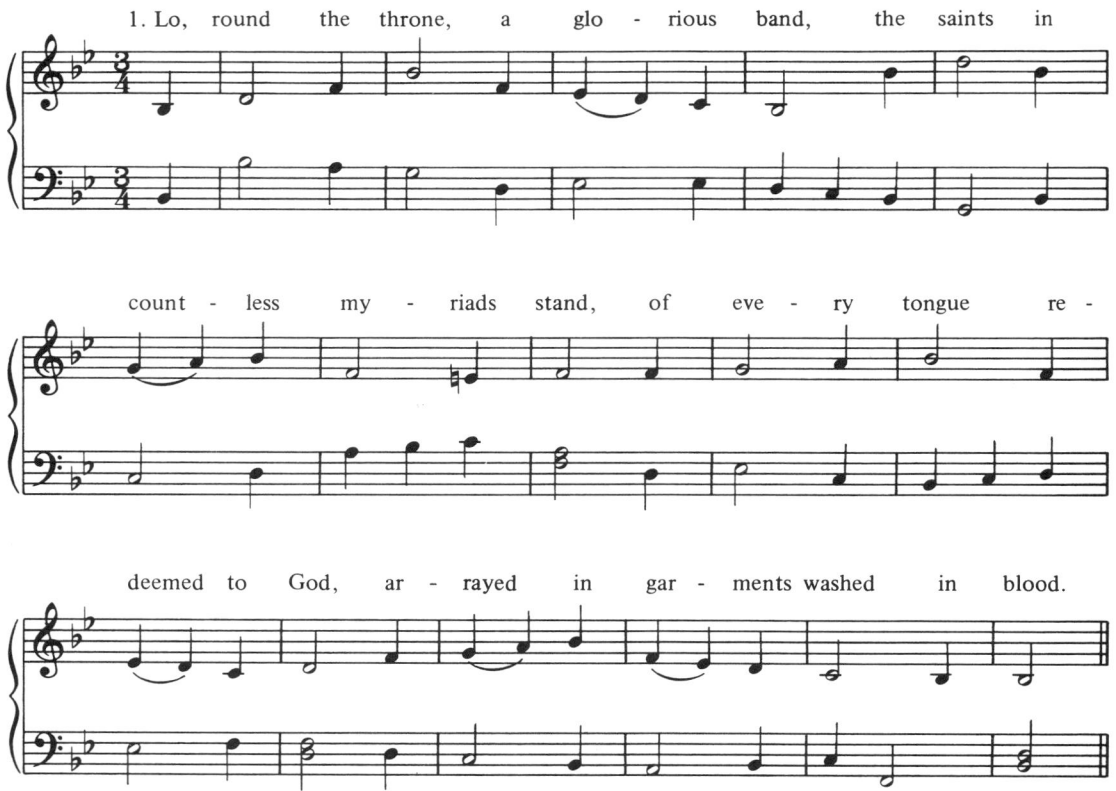

2. Through tribulation great they came;
   they bore the cross, despised the shame;
   from all their labours now they rest,
   in God's eternal glory blest.

3. They see their Saviour face to face,
   and sing the triumphs of his grace;
   him day and night they ceaseless praise,
   to him the loud thanksgiving raise:

4. 'Worthy the Lamb, for sinners slain,
   through endless years to live and reign;
   thou hast redeemed us by thy blood,
   and made us kings and priests to God.'

5. O may we tread the sacred road
   that saints and holy martyrs trod;
   wage to the end the glorious strife,
   and win, like them, a crown of life.

DEUS, TUORUM MILITUM L.M.
Text: Rowland Hill (1744-1833) and others   Music: Melody from *Grenoble Antiphoner* (1753)

58 Love divine, all loves excelling

1. Love di - vine, all loves ex - cell- ing, joy of heaven, to earth come down, fix in us thy hum - ble dwell - ing, all thy faith - ful mer - cies crown.

2. Jesus, thou art all compassion,
   pure unbounded love thou art;
   visit us with thy salvation,
   enter every trembling heart.

3. Come, almighty to deliver,
   let us all thy life receive;
   suddenly return, and never,
   never more thy temples leave.

4. Thee we would be always blessing,
   serve thee as thy hosts above;
   pray, and praise thee without ceasing,
   glory in thy perfect love.

5. Finish then thy new creation,
   pure and sinless let us be;
   let us see thy great salvation
   perfectly restored in thee.

6. Changed from glory into glory
   till in heaven we take our place,
   till we cast our crowns before thee,
   lost in wonder, love, and praise.

LOVE DIVINE 8 7. 8 7.
Text: Charles Wesley (1707-1788) Music: John Stainer (1840-1901)

59 Majesty, worship his majesty

Text and Music: Jack Hayford

60 Make me a channel of your peace

Text and Music: Sebastian Temple

Dedicated to Mrs Frances Tracy

61 Morning has broken

2. Sweet the rain's new fall sunlit from heaven.
   like the first dew-fall on the first grass.
   Praise for the sweetness of the wet garden,
   sprung in completeness where his feet pass.

3. Mine is the sunlight! Mine is the morning
   born of the one light Eden saw play!
   Praise with elation, praise every morning,
   God's re-creation of the new day!

BUNESSAN 5 5. 5 4. D.
Text: Eleanor Farjeon (1881-1965) Music: Traditional Gaelic Melody

62 My song is love unknown

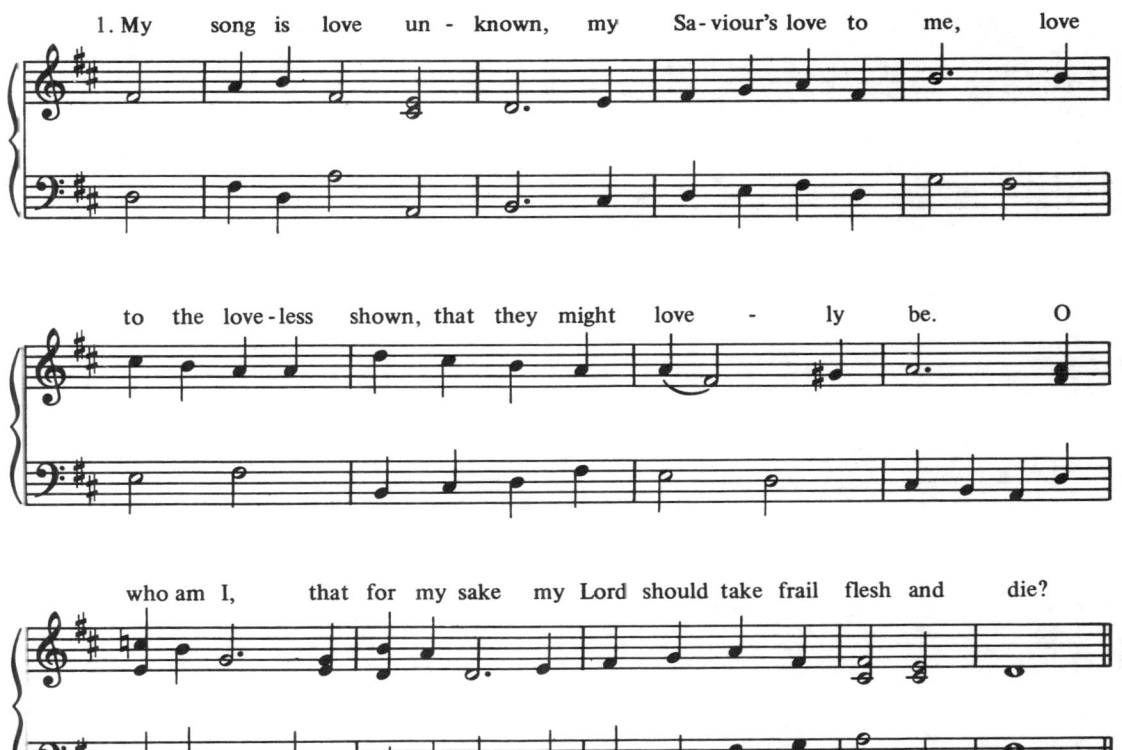

1. My song is love un-known, my Sa-viour's love to me, love
to the love-less shown, that they might love - ly be. O
who am I, that for my sake my Lord should take frail flesh and die?

2. He came from his blest throne,
salvation to bestow;
but men made strange, and none
the longed-for Christ would know.
But O, my friend, my friend indeed,
who at my need
his life did spend!

3. Sometimes they strew his way,
and his sweet praises sing;
resounding all the day
hosannas to their King.
Then 'Crucify!' is all their breath,
and for his death they thirst and cry.

4. Why, what hath my Lord done?
What makes this rage and spite?
He made the lame to run,
he gave the blind their sight.
Sweet injuries! yet they at these
themselves displease,
and 'gainst him rise.

5. They rise, and needs will have
my dear Lord made away;
a murderer they save,
the Prince of Life they slay.
Yet cheerful he to suffering goes,
that he his foes
from thence might free.

6. In life, no house, no home
my Lord on earth might have;
in death, no friendly tomb
but what a stranger gave.
What may I say? Heaven was his home;
but mine the tomb wherein he lay.

7. Here might I stay and sing;
no story so divine;
never was love, dear King,
never was grief like thine!
This is my friend, in whose sweet praise
I all my days
could gladly spend.

LOVE UNKNOWN 6 6. 6 6. 4 4. 4 4.
Text: Samuel Crossman (1624-1683)   Music: John Ireland (1879-1962)

63 Now thank we all our God

2. O may this bounteous God
through all our life be near us,
with ever joyful hearts
and blessèd peace to cheer us;
and keep us in his grace,
and guide us when perplexed,
and free us from all ills
in this world and the next.

3. All praise and thanks to God
the Father now be given,
the Son, and him who reigns
with them in highest heaven,
the one eternal God,
whom earth and heaven adore,
for thus it was, is now,
and shall be evermore.

NUN DANKET 6 7. 6 7. 6 6. 6 6.
Text: Martin Rinkart (1586-1649), translated by Catherine Winkworth (1827-1878)
Music: Johann Crüger (1598-1662)

64 O come, O come, Emmanuel

Verse

1. O come, O come, Em - man - u - el, and ran - som cap - tive Is - ra - el, that mourns in lone - ly ex - ile here, un - til the Son of God ap - pear:

Chorus

Re - joice, re - joice! Em - man - u - el shall come to thee, O Is - ra - el.

2. O come, thou Rod of Jesse, free
   thine own from Satan's tyranny;
   from depths of hell thy people save,
   and give them victory o'er the grave:

3. O come, thou Dayspring, come and cheer
   our spirits by thine advent here;
   disperse the gloomy clouds of night,
   and death's dark shadows put to flight:

4. O come, thou Key of David. come,
   and open wide our heavenly home;
   make safe the way that leads on high,
   and close the path to misery:

5. O come, O come, thou Lord of Might,
   who to thy tribes, on Sinai's height,
   in ancient times, didst give the law
   in cloud and majesty and awe:

VENI EMMANUEL 8 8. 8 8. 8 8.
Text: Translated from the Latin by John Mason Neale (1818-1866)
Music: Adapted from a French Missal by Thomas Helmore (1811-1890)

65 O God of Bethel

1. O God of Beth - el, by whose hand thy

peo - ple still are fed, who through this wea - ry

pil - grim - age hast all our fa - thers led;

2. Our vows, our prayers, we now present
   before thy throne of grace;
   God of our fathers, be the God
   of their succeeding race.

3. Through each perplexing path of life
   our wandering footsteps guide;
   give us each day our daily bread,
   and raiment fit provide.

4. O spread thy covering wings around,
   till all our wanderings cease,
   and at our Father's loved abode
   our souls arrive in peace.

MARTYRDOM C.M.
Text: Philip Doddridge (1702-1751) Music: Hugh Wilson (1766-1824)

66 O God our help in ages past

1. O God, our help in a-ges past, our hope for years to come, our
shel - ter from the stor - my blast, and our e - ter - nal home.

2. Beneath the shadow of thy throne
   thy saints have dwelt secure;
   sufficient is thine arm alone,
   and our defence is sure.

3. Before the hills in order stood,
   or earth received her frame,
   from everlasting thou art God,
   to endless years the same.

4. A thousand ages in thy sight
   are like an evening gone;
   short as the watch that ends the night
   before the rising sun.

5. Time, like an ever-rolling stream,
   bears all its sons away;
   they fly forgotten, as a dream
   dies at the opening day.

6. O God, our help in ages past,
   our hope for years to come,
   be thou our guard while troubles last,
   and our eternal home.

ST ANNE C.M.
Text: Isaac Watts (1674-1748)
Music: Melody from *A Supplement to the New Version* (1708), probably by William Croft (1678-1727)

67 O Lord, my God

2. And when I think that God, his Son not sparing,
   sent him to die, I scarce can take it in
   that on the cross, my burden gladly bearing,
   he bled and died to take away my sin.

3. When Christ shall come with shout of acclamation
   and take me home, what joy shall fill my heart;
   when I shall bow in humble adoration,
   and there proclaim my God, how great thou art.

Text: Karl Boberg, translated by Stuart K Hine   Music: Swedish Folk Melody

68 O praise ye the Lord!

2. O praise ye the Lord! praise him upon earth,
   in tuneful accord, ye sons of new birth;
   praise him who hath brought you his grace from above,
   praise him who hath taught you to sing of his love.

3. O praise ye the Lord, all things that give sound;
   each jubilant chord re-echo around;
   loud organs his glory forth tell in deep tone,
   and sweet harp the story of what he hath done.

4. O praise ye the Lord! thanksgiving and song
   to him be outpoured all ages along:
   for love in creation, for heaven restored,
   for grace of salvation, O praise ye the Lord!

LAUDATE DOMINUM 10 10. 11 11.
Text: Henry William Baker (1821-1877) Music: Charles Hubert Hastings Parry (1848-1918)

69 O sacred head

1. O sa-cred head, sur-round-ed by crown of pierc-ing thorn! O bleed-ing head, so wound-ed, so shamed and put to scorn! Death's pal-lid hue comes o'er thee, the glow of life de-cays; yet an-gel hosts a-dore thee, and trem-ble as they gaze.

2. Thy comeliness and vigour
   is withered up and gone,
   and in thy wasted figure
   I see death drawing on.
   O agony and dying!
   O love to sinners free!
   Jesu, all grace supplying,
   turn thou thy face on me.

3. In this thy bitter passion,
   good shepherd, think of me
   with thy most sweet compassion,
   unworthy though I be:
   beneath thy cross abiding
   for ever would I rest,
   in thy dear love confiding,
   and with thy presence blest.

PASSION CHORALE 7 6. 7 6. D.
Text: Paul Gerhardt (1607-1676), based on *Salve caput cruentatum*,
translated by Henry William Baker (1821-1877) Music: Hans Leo Hassler (1564-1612)

70 O worship the King

1. O wor-ship the King all glo-rious a-bove; O grate-ful-ly sing his power and his love; our shield and de-fen-der, the an-cient of days, pa-vi-lioned in splen-dour and gird-ed with praise.

2. O tell of his might, O sing of his grace,
   whose robe is the light, whose canopy space;
   his chariots of wrath the deep thunder clouds
   form,
   and dark is his path on the wings of the storm.

3. The earth with its store of wonders untold,
   almighty, thy power hath founded of old;
   hath 'stablished it fast by a changeless decree,
   and round it hath cast, like a mantle, the sea.

4. Thy bountiful care what tongue can recite?
   it breathes in the air, it shines in the light;
   it streams from the hills, it descends to the
   plain,
   and sweetly distils in the dew and the rain.

5. Frail children of dust and feeble as frail,
   in thee do we trust, nor find thee to fail;
   thy mercies how tender, how firm to the end!
   our maker, defender, redeemer, and friend.

6. O measureless might, ineffable love,
   while angels delight to hymn thee above,
   thy humbler creation, though feeble their lays,
   with true adoration shall sing to thy praise.

HANOVER 10 10. 11 11.
Text: Robert Grant (1779-1838) Music: William Croft (1687-1727)

71 O worship the Lord

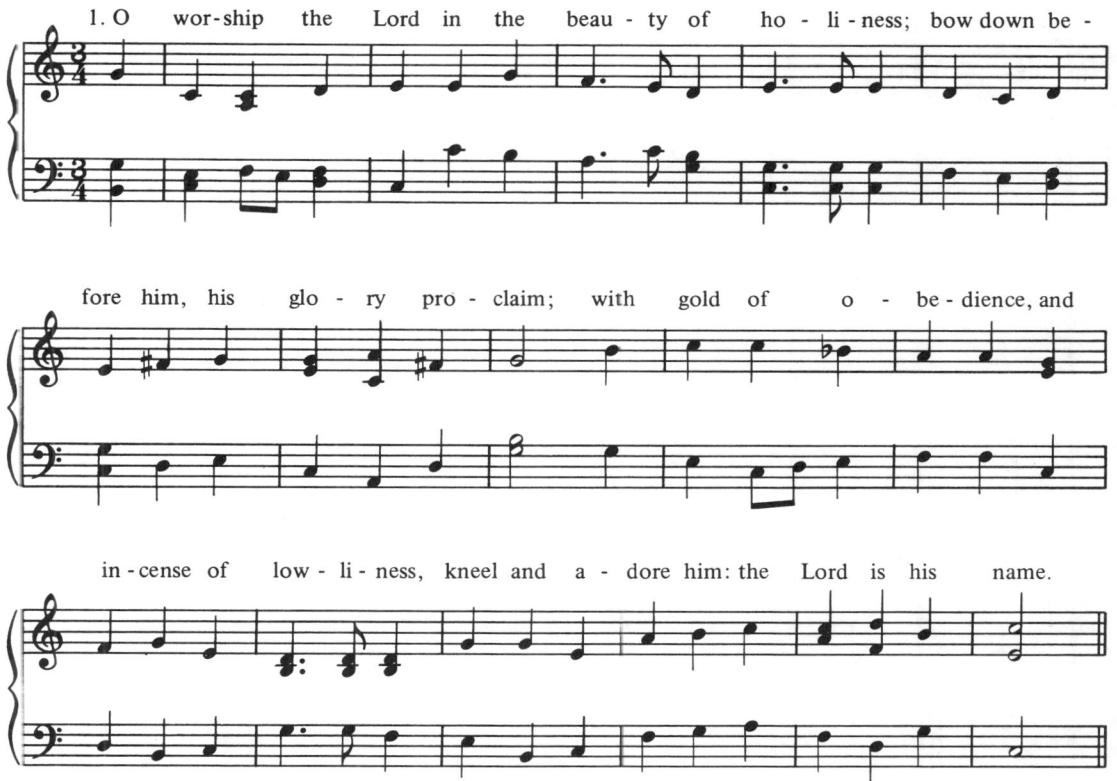

1. O worship the Lord in the beauty of holiness; bow down before him, his glory proclaim; with gold of obedience, and incense of lowliness, kneel and adore him: the Lord is his name.

2. Low at his feet lay thy burden of carefulness:
   high on his heart he will bear it for thee,
   comfort thy sorrows, and answer thy prayerfulness,
   guiding thy steps as may best for thee be.

3. Fear not to enter his courts in the slenderness
   of the poor wealth thou wouldst reckon as thine:
   truth in its beauty, and love in its tenderness,
   these are the offerings to lay on his shrine.

4. These, though we bring them in trembling and fearfulness,
   he will accept for the name that is dear;
   mornings of joy give for evenings of tearfulness,
   trust for our trembling and hope for our fear.

WAS LEBET 13 10. 13 10.
Text: John Samuel Bewley Monsell (1811-1875) Music: Melody from *Rheinhardt* MS, Üttingen (1754)

72 On a hill far away *(The old rugged cross)*

I will cling to the old rug-ged cross

and ex-change it some-day for a crown.

2. Oh that old rugged cross, so despised by the world,
   has a wondrous attraction for me:
   for the dear Lamb of God left his glory above
   to bear it to dark Calvary.

3. In the old rugged cross, stained with blood so divine,
   a wondrous beauty I see.
   For 'twas on that old cross Jesus suffered and died
   to pardon and sanctify me.

4. To the old rugged cross I will ever be true, its shame and reproach gladly bear.
   Then he'll call me some day to my home far away;
   there his glory for ever I'll share.

Text and Music: George Bennard

73 On Jordan's bank

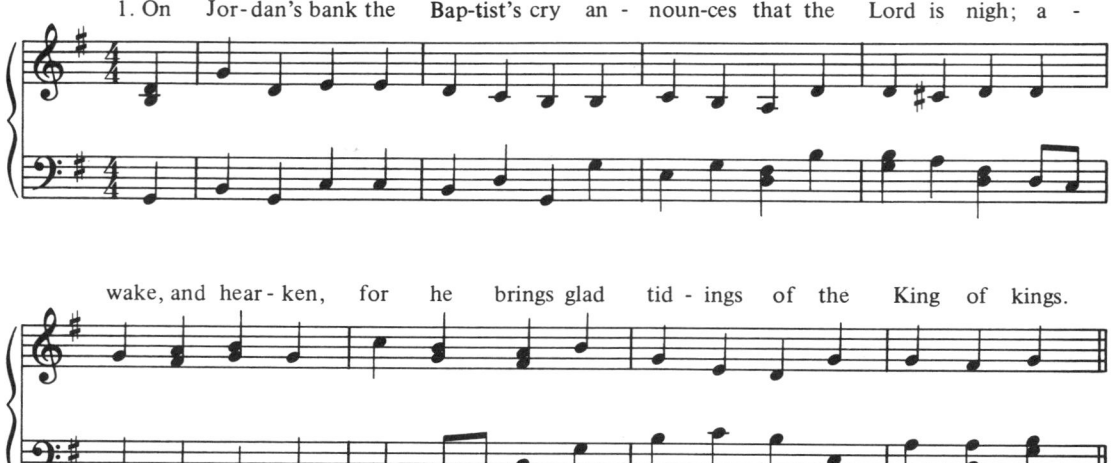

1. On Jor-dan's bank the Bap-tist's cry an - noun-ces that the Lord is nigh; a - wake, and hear - ken, for he brings glad tid - ings of the King of kings.

2. Then cleansed be every breast from sin;
   make straight the way for God within;
   prepare we in our hearts a home,
   where such a mighty guest may come.

3. For thou art our salvation, Lord,
   our refuge, and our great reward;
   without thy grace we waste away,
   like flowers that wither and decay.

4. To heal the sick stretch out thine hand,
   and bid the fallen sinner stand;
   shine forth, and let thy light restore
   earth's own true loveliness once more.

5. All praise, eternal Son, to thee
   whose advent doth thy people free,
   whom with the Father we adore
   and Holy Ghost for evermore.

WINCHESTER NEW L. M.
Text: Charles Coffin (1676-1749), translated by John Chandler (1806-1876)
Music: From *Musikalisch Handbuch*, Hamburg (1690)

74 Open our eyes, Lord

Text and Music: Robert Cull

75 Peace is flowing like a river

2. Love is flowing like a river,
   flowing out through you and me,
   spreading out into the desert,
   setting all the captives free.

3. Joy is flowing like a river,
   flowing out through you and me,
   spreading out into the desert,
   setting all the captives free.

4. Hope is flowing like a river,
   flowing out through you and me,
   spreading out into the desert,
   setting all the captives free.

Text and Music: Traditional

76 Praise my soul

1. Praise, my soul, the King of hea - ven, to his feet thy tri - bute bring; ran-somed, healed, re - stored, for - gi - ven, who like me his praise should sing? Al - le - lu - ia, al - le - lu - ia, praise the ev - er - last - ing King.

2. Praise him for his grace and favour
   to our fathers in distress;
   praise him still the same as ever,
   slow to chide, and swift to bless:
   alleluia, alleluia,
   glorious in his faithfulness.

3. Father-like, he tends and spares us,
   well our feeble frame he knows;
   in his hands he gently bears us,
   rescues us from all our foes:
   alleluia, alleluia,
   widely as his mercy flows.

4. Angels, help us to adore him;
   ye behold him face to face;
   sun and moon, bow down before him,
   dwellers all in time and space:
   alleluia, alleluia,
   praise with us the God of grace.

PRAISE MY SOUL 8 7. 8 7. 8 7.
Text: Henry Francis Lyte (1793-1847)
Music: John Goss (1800-1880)

77 Praise the Lord!

1. Praise the Lord! Ye heav'ns a - dore him, praise him, an - gels in the height; sun and moon, re - joice be - fore him, praise him, all ye stars and light, Praise the Lord, for he is glo - rious; worlds his migh - ty voice o - beyed: laws, which ne - ver shall be bro - ken, for their gui - dance he hath made.

2. Praise the Lord! for he is glorious;
   never shall his promise fail;
   God hath made his saints victorious;
   sin and death shall not prevail.
   Praise the God of our salvation,
   hosts on high, his power proclaim,
   heaven and earth and all creation,
   laud and magnify his name!

3. Worship, honour, glory, blessing,
   Lord, we offer to thy name;
   young and old, thy praise expressing,
   join their Saviour to proclaim.
   As the saints in heaven adore thee,
   we would bow before thy throne;
   as thine angels serve before thee,
   so on earth thy will be done.

AUSTRIA 8 7. 8 7. D.
Text: Verse 1-2 from the *Foundling Hospital Collection* (1796) Verse 3 by Edward Osler (1798-1863)
Music: Franz Joseph Haydn (1732-1809)

78 Praise to the holiest

1. Praise to the Holiest in the height, and in the depth be praise: in all his words most wonderful, most sure in all his ways.

2. O loving wisdom of our God!
when all was sin and shame,
a second Adam to the fight
and to the rescue came.

3. O wisest love! that flesh and blood,
which did in Adam fail,
should strive afresh against the foe,
should strive and should prevail;

4. and that a higher gift than grace
should flesh and blood refine,
God's presence and his very self,
and essence all-divine.

5. O generous love! that he, who smote
in Man for man the foe,
the double agony in Man
for man should undergo;

6. and in he garden secretly,
and on the cross on high,
should teach his brethren, and inspire
to suffer and to die.

7. Praise to the Holiest in the hieght,
and in the depth be praise:
in all his words most wonderful,
most sure in all his ways.

GERONTIUS C. M.
Text: John Henry Newman (1801-1890) Music: John Bacchus Dykes (1823-1876)

79 Praise to the Lord, the Almighty

1. Praise to the Lord, the Al-might-y, the King of cre-a-tion; O my soul, praise him for he is thy health and sal-va-tion: all ye who hear, now to his tem-ple draw near, join-ing in glad a-dor-a-tion.

2. Praise to the Lord, who o'er all things so wondrously reigneth,
   shieldeth thee gently from harm, or when fainting sustaineth:
   hast thou not seen how thy heart's wishes have been
   granted in what he ordaineth?

3. Praise to the Lord, who doth prosper thy work and defend thee;
   surely his goodness and mercy shall daily attend thee:
   ponder anew what the Almighty can do,
   if to the end he befriend thee.

4. Praise to the Lord! O let all that is in me adore him!
   All that hath life and breath, come now with praises before him!
   let the Amen sound from his people again:
   gladly for aye we adore him.

LOBE DEN HERREN 14 14. 4 7. 8.
Text: Joachim Neander (1650-1680), translated by Catherine Winkworth (1827-1878)
Music: German Melody (17c.), composer unknown

80 Rejoice! the Lord is King

Verse

1. Re - joice! the Lord is King. Your Lord and King a - dore; mor-tals, give thanks and sing, and tri - umph ev - er - more. Lift up your heart, lift up your voice; re - joice, a - gain I say, re - joice.

Chorus

2. Jesus, the Saviour, reigns,
   the God of truth and love;
   when he had purged our stains,
   he took his seat above.

3. His kingdom cannot fail;
   he rules o'er earth and heaven;
   the keys of death and hell
   are to our Jesus given.

4. He sits at God's right hand
   till all his foes submit,
   and bow to his command,
   and fall beneath his feet.

GOPSAL 6 6. 6 6. 8 8.
Text: Charles Wesley (1707-1788) Music: George Frideric Handel (1685-1759)

81 Seek ye first

2. Ask and it shall be given unto you,
   seek and ye shall find;
   knock, and it shall be opened unto you;
   allelu, alleluia.
   Alleluia, alleluia, alleluia, allelu, alleluia.

Text and Music: Karen Lafferty

82 Spirit of the living God

1. Spirit of the living God, fall a-fresh on me.
Spirit of the living God, fall a-fresh on me.
Melt me, mould me, fill me, use me.
Spirit of the living God, fall a-fresh on me.

2. Repeat verse 1 singing 'us' instead of 'me'.

*When appropriate, a third verse may be
added, singing 'on them' – for example,
before Confirmation, or at a service for the sick.*

Text and Music: Daniel Iverson

83 The advent of our King

1. The advent of our King our prayers must now employ, and
we must hymns of welcome sing in strains of holy joy.

2. The everlasting Son
   incarnate deigns to be;
   himself a servant's form puts on,
   to set his servants free.

3. Daughter of Sion, rise
   to meet thy lowly King;
   nor let thy faithless heart despise
   the peace he comes to bring.

4. As Judge, on clouds of light,
   he soon will come again,
   and his true members all unite
   with him in heaven to reign.

5. All glory to the Son
   who comes to set us free,
   with Father, Spirit, ever One,
   through all eternity.

FRANCONIA S. M.
Text: Charles Coffin (1676-1749), translated by John Chandler (1806-1876)
Music: From König's *Harmonischer Lieder-Schatz* (1738), adapted by William Henry Havergal (1793-1870)

84 The Church's one foundation

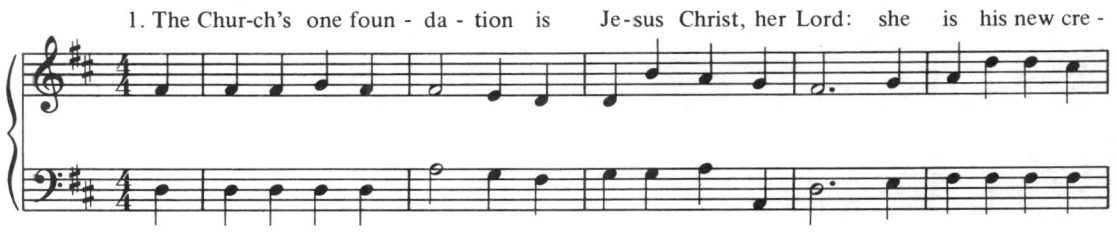

1. The Church's one foundation is Jesus Christ, her Lord: she is his new cre -

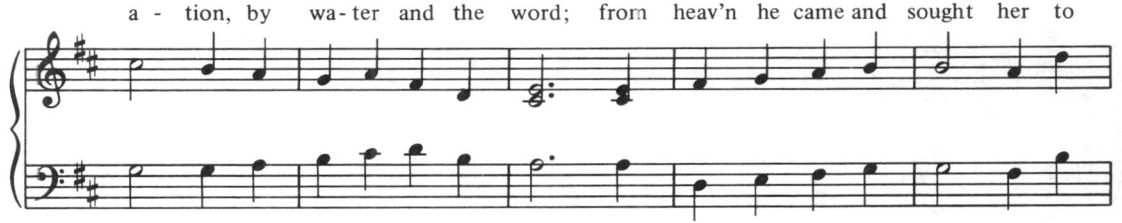

a - tion, by water and the word; from heav'n he came and sought her to

be his holy bride, with his own blood he bought her, and for her life he died.

2. Elect from every nation,
   yet one o'er all the earth,
   her charter of salvation
   one Lord, one faith, one birth;
   one holy name she blesses,
   partakes one holy food,
   and to one hope she presses,
   with every grace endued.

3. 'Mid toil, and tribulation,
   and tumult of her war,
   she waits the consummation
   of peace for evermore;
   till with the vision glorious
   her longing eyes are blest,
   and the great Church victorious
   shall be the Church at rest.

4. Yet she on earth hath union
   with God the Three in One,
   and mystic sweet communion
   with those whose rest is won:
   O happy ones and holy!
   Lord, give us grace that we
   like them, the meek and lowly,
   on high may dwell with thee.

AURELIA 7 6. 7 6. D.
Text: Samuel John Stone (1830-1900)
Music: Samuel Sebastian Wesley (1810-1876)

85 The day of resurrection!

2. Our hearts be pure from evil,
   that we may see aright
   the Lord in rays eternal
   of resurrection-light;
   and, listening to his accents,
   may hear so calm and plain
   his own 'All hail,' and, hearing,
   may raise the victor strain.

3. Now let the heavens be joyful,
   and earth her song begin,
   the round world keep high triumph,
   and all that is therein;
   let all things seen and unseen
   their notes of gladness blend,
   for Christ the Lord is risen,
   our joy that hath no end.

ELLACOMBE 7 6. 7 6. D.
Text: St. John of Damascus (d. c.754), translated by John Mason Neale (1818-1866)
Music: Melody from *Württemberg Gesangbuch* (1784)

86 The day thou gavest

1. The day thou gav - est, Lord, is end - ed, the dark - ness falls at thy be - hest; to thee our morn - ing hymns as - cend - ed, thy praise shall sanc - ti - fy our rest.

2. We thank thee that thy Church unsleeping,
while earth rolls onward into light,
through all the world her watch is keeping,
and rests not now by day or night.

3. As o'er each continent and island
the dawn leads on another day,
the voice of prayer is never silent,
nor dies the strain of praise away.

4. The sun that bids us rest is waking
our brethren 'neath the western sky,
and hour by hour fresh lips are making
thy wondrous doings heard on high.

5. So be it, Lord; thy throne shall never,
like earth's proud empires, pass away;
thy kingdom stands, and grows for ever,
till all thy creatures own thy sway.

ST CLEMENT 9 8. 9 8.
Text: John Ellerton (1826-1893) Music: Clement Cotterill Scholefield (1839-1904)

87 The head that once was crowned

1. The head that once was crowned with thorns is crowned with glo-ry now: a roy-al di-a-dem a-dorns the migh-ty vic-tor's brow.

2. The highest place that heaven affords
   is his, is his by right,
   the King of kings, and Lord of lords,
   and heaven's eternal light;

3. The joy of all who dwell above,
   the joy of all below,
   to whom he manifests his love,
   and grants his name to know.

4. To them the cross, with all its shame,
   with all its grace, is given:
   their name an everlasting name,
   their joy the joy of heaven.

5. They suffer with their Lord below,
   they reign with him above;
   their profit and their joy to know
   the mystery of his love.

6. The cross he bore is life and health,
   though shame and death to him;
   his people's hope, his people's wealth,
   their everlasting theme.

ST MAGNUS C. M.
Text: Thomas Kelly (1769-1855)   Music: Jeremiah Clarke (c.1673-1707)

88 The heavenly child in stature grows

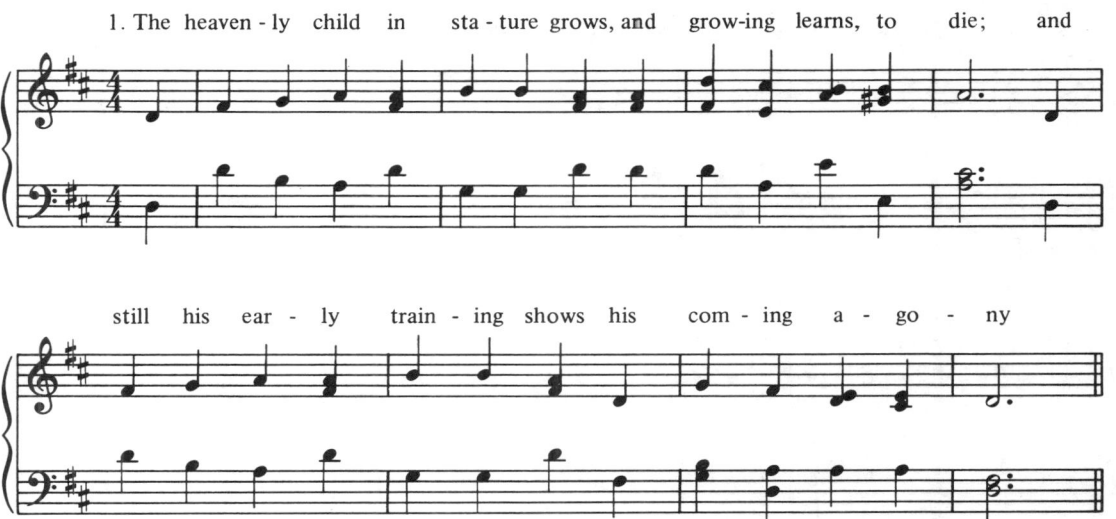

1. The heaven-ly child in sta-ture grows, and grow-ing learns, to die; and still his ear-ly train-ing shows his com-ing a-go-ny

2. The Son of God his glory hides
   to dwell with parents poor;
   and he who made the heavens abides
   in dwelling-place obscure.

3. Those mighty hands that rule the sky
   no earthly toil refuse;
   the maker of the stars on high
   an humble trade pursues.

4. He whom the choirs of angels praise,
   bearing each dread decree,
   his earthly parents now obeys
   in glad humility.

5. For this thy lowliness revealed,
   Jesu, we thee adore,
   and praise to God the Father yield
   and Spirit evermore.

TALLIS'S ORDINAL C. M.
Text: J. B. de Santeuil (1630-1697), translated by John Chandler (1806-1876)
Music: Thomas Tallis (c.1505-1585)

89 The King of Love my shepherd is

1. The King of love my shep-herd is, whose good-ness fail-eth ne-ver; I no-thing lack if I am his, and he is mine for e - ver.

2. Where streams of living water flow
   my ransomed soul he leadeth,
   and where the verdant pastures grow
   with food celestial feedeth.

3. Perverse and foolish oft I strayed,
   but yet in love he sought me,
   and on his shoulder gently laid,
   and home rejoicing brought me.

4. In death's dark vale I fear no ill
   with thee, dear Lord, beside me;
   thy rod and staff my comfort still,
   thy cross before to guide me.

5. Thou spread'st a table in my sight;
   thy unction grace bestoweth;
   and O what transport of delight
   from thy pure chalice floweth!

6. And so through all the length of days
   thy goodness faileth never:
   good Shepherd, may I sing thy praise
   within thy house for ever.

DOMINUS REGIT ME 8 7. 8 7.
Text: Henry Williams Baker (1821-1877) Music: John Bacchus Dykes (1823-1876)

90 The Lord's my shepherd

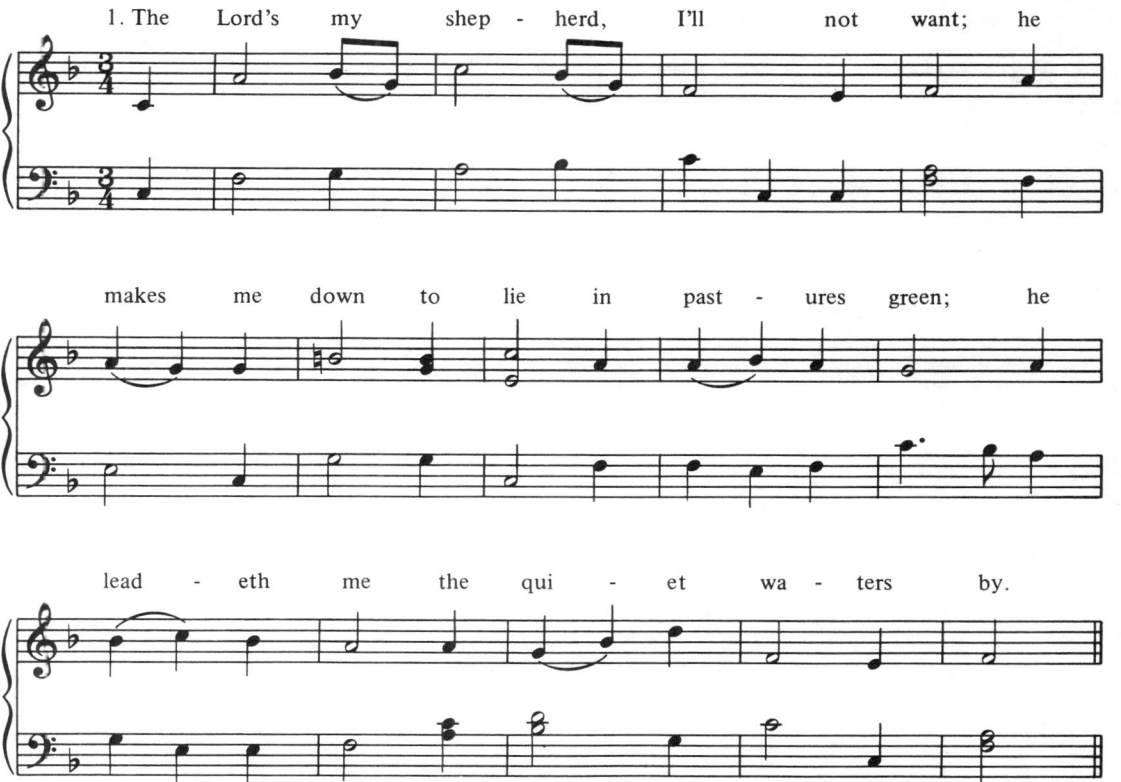

1. The Lord's my shep - herd, I'll not want; he
makes me down to lie in past - ures green; he
lead - eth me the qui - et wa - ters by.

2. My soul he doth restore again,
   and me to walk doth make
   within the paths of righteousness,
   e'en for his own name's sake.

3. Yea, though I walk in death's dark vale,
   yet will I fear none ill.
   For thou art with me, and thy rod
   and staff me comfort still.

4. My table thou hast furnishèd
   in presence of my foes,
   my head thou dost with oil anoint,
   and my cup overflows.

5. Goodness and mercy all my life
   shall surely follow me.
   And in God's house for evermore
   my dwelling place shall be.

CRIMOND C.M.
Text: Paraphrased from Psalm 22(23) in the *Scottish Psalter* (1650)
Music: Jessie Seymour Irvine (1836-1887)

91 The race that long in darkness pined

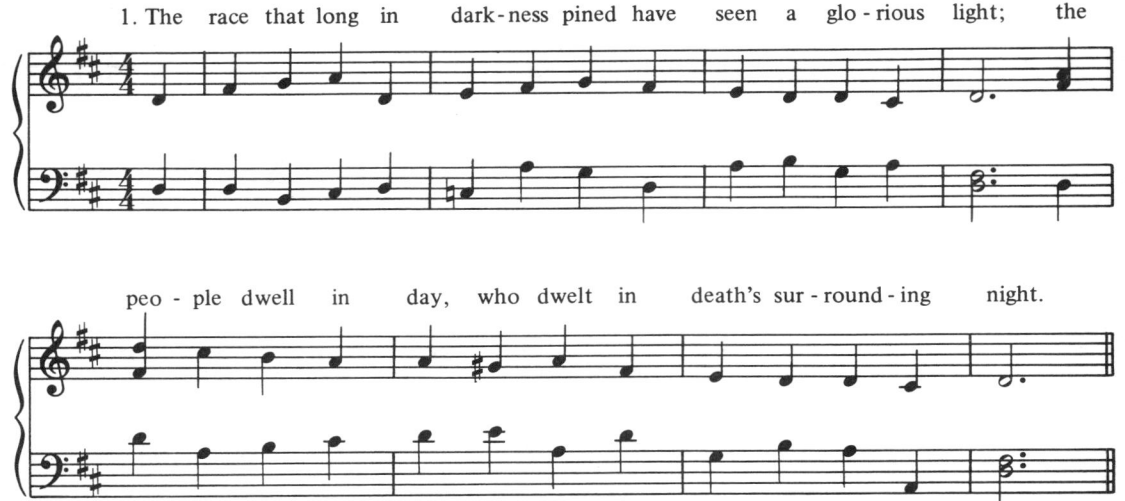

1. The race that long in darkness pined have seen a glorious light; the people dwell in day, who dwelt in death's surrounding night.

2. To hail thy rise, thou better sun,
   the gathering nations come,
   joyous as when the reapers bear
   the harvest-treasures home.

3. To us a child of hope is born,
   to us a Son is given;
   him shall the tribes of earth obey,
   him all the hosts of heaven.

4. His name shall be the Prince of Peace,
   for evermore adored;
   the Wonderful, the Counsellor,
   the great and mighty Lord.

5. His power increasing still shall spread;
   his reign no end shall know:
   justice shall guard his throne above,
   and peace abound below.

DUNDEE C. M.
Text: John Morison (1750-1798)   Music: Melody from the *Scottish Psalter*, (1615)

92 Thine be the glory

Verse

1. Thine be the glory, ri - sen, conquering son, endless is the victory thou o'er death hast won; an - gels in bright rai - ment rolled the stone a - way, kept the fold-ed grave clothes where thy bo - dy lay.

Chorus

Thine be the glory, ri - sen, conquering son, end - less is the vic - tory thou o'er death hast won.

2. Lo, Jesus meets us, risen from the tomb;
   lovingly he greets us, scatters fear and gloom;
   let the Church with gladness hymns of triumph sing,
   for her Lord now liveth, death hath lost its sting:

3. No more we doubt thee, glorious Prince of Life;
   life is nought without thee: aid us in our strife;
   make us more than conquerors through thy deathless love;
   bring us safe through Jordan to thy home above:

MACCABAEUS 10 11. 11 11.
Text: Edmond Budry (1854-1932), translated by Richard Birch Hoyle (1875-1939)
Music: George Frideric Handel (1685-1759)

93 Thou, whose almighty word

1. Thou, whose al - migh - ty word cha - os and dark - ness heard, and took their flight; hear us, we hum - bly pray, and where the gos - pel day sheds not its glo - rious ray let there be light.

2. Thou, who didst come to bring
on thy redeeming wing
healing and sight,
health to the sick in mind,
sight to the inly blind,
O now to all mankind
let there be light.

3. Spirit of truth and love,
life-giving, holy Dove,
speed forth thy flight;
move on the water's face,
bearing the lamp of grace,
and in earth's darkest place
let there be light.

4. Holy and blessed Three,
glorious Trinity,
Wisdom, Love, Might;
boundless as ocean's tide
rolling in fullest pride,
through the earth far and wide
let there be light.

MOSCOW 6 6 4. 6 6 6 4.
Text: John Marriott (1780-1825) Music: Felice de Giardini (1716-1796)

94 Thy hand, O God, has guided

2. Thy heralds brought glad tidings
   to greatest, as to least;
   they bade men rise, and hasten
   to share the great King's feast;
   and this was all their teaching,
   in every deed and word,
   to all alike proclaiming
   one Church, one faith, one Lord.

3. When shadows thick were falling,
   and all seemed sunk in night,
   thou, Lord, didst send thy servants,
   thy chosen sons of light.
   On them and on thy people
   thy plenteous grace was poured,
   and this was still their message:
   one Church, one faith, one Lord.

4. Through many a day of darkness,
   through many a scene of strife,
   the faithful few fought bravely,
   to guard the nation's life.
   Their gospel of redemption,
   sin pardoned, man restored,
   was all in this enfolded:
   one Church, one faith, one Lord.

5. And we, shall we be faithless?
   shall hearts fail, hands hang down?
   shall we evade the conflict,
   and cast away our crown?
   Not so: in God's deep counsels
   some better thing is stored;
   we will maintain unflinching,
   one Church, one faith, one Lord.

6. Thy mercy will not fail us,
   nor leave thy work undone;
   with thy right hand to help us,
   the victory shall be won;
   and then, by men and angels,
   thy name shall be adored,
   and this shall be their anthem:
   one Church, one faith, one Lord.

THORNBURY 7 6. 7 6. D.
Text: Edward Hayes Plumptre (1821-1891) Music: Basil Harwood (1859-1949)

95 We have a gospel to proclaim

1. We have a gospel to proclaim, good news for men in all the earth; the gospel of a Saviour's name: we sing his glory, tell his worth.

2. Tell of his birth at Bethlehem
not in a royal house or hall
but in a stable dark and dim,
the Word made flesh, a light for all.

3. Tell of his death at Calvary,
hated by those he came to save,
in lonely suffering on the cross;
for all he loved his life he gave.

4. Tell of that glorious Easter morn:
empty the tomb, for he was free.
He broke the power of death and hell
that we might share his victory.

5. Tell of his reign at God's right hand,
by all creation glorified.
He sends his Spirit on his Church
to live for him, the Lamb who died.

6. Now we rejoice to name him King:
Jesus is Lord of all the earth.
The gospel-message we proclaim:
we sing his glory, tell his worth.

FULDA L. M.
Text: Edward Joseph Burns (b.1938)   Music: From William Gardiner's *Sacred Melodies* (1815)

96 We plough the fields, and scatter

thank the Lord, O thank the Lord, for all his love.

2. He only is the maker,
   of all things near and far;
   he paints the wayside flower,
   he lights the evening star;
   the winds and waves obey him,
   by him the birds are fed;
   much more, to us his children,
   he gives our daily bread.

3. We thank thee then, O Father,
   for all things bright and good,
   the seed-time and the harvest,
   our life, our health, our food.
   Accept the gifts we offer
   for all thy love imparts,
   and, what thou most desirest,
   our humble, thankful hearts.

WIR PFLÜGEN 7 6. 7 6. D. 6 6. 8 4.
Text: Matthias Claudius (1740-1815), translated by Jane Montgomery Campbell (1817-1878)
Music: Johann Abraham Peter Schulz (1747-1800)

97 When I survey the wondrous cross

1. When I survey the wond-rous cross on which the Prince of Glory died, my rich-est gain I count but loss, and pour con-tempt on all my pride.

2. Forbid it, Lord, that I should boast
   save in the cross of Christ my God;
   all the vain things that charm me most,
   I sacrifice them to his blood.

3. See from his head, his hands, his feet,
   sorrow and love flow mingling down;
   did e'er such love and sorrow meet,
   or thorns compose so rich a crown?

4. Were the whole realm of nature mine,
   that were an offering far too small;
   love so amazing, so divine,
   demands my soul, my life, my all.

ROCKINGHAM L.M.
Text: Isaac Watts (1674-1748)   Music: Composer unknown, adapted by Edward Miller (1731-1807)

98 Ye choirs of new Jerusalem

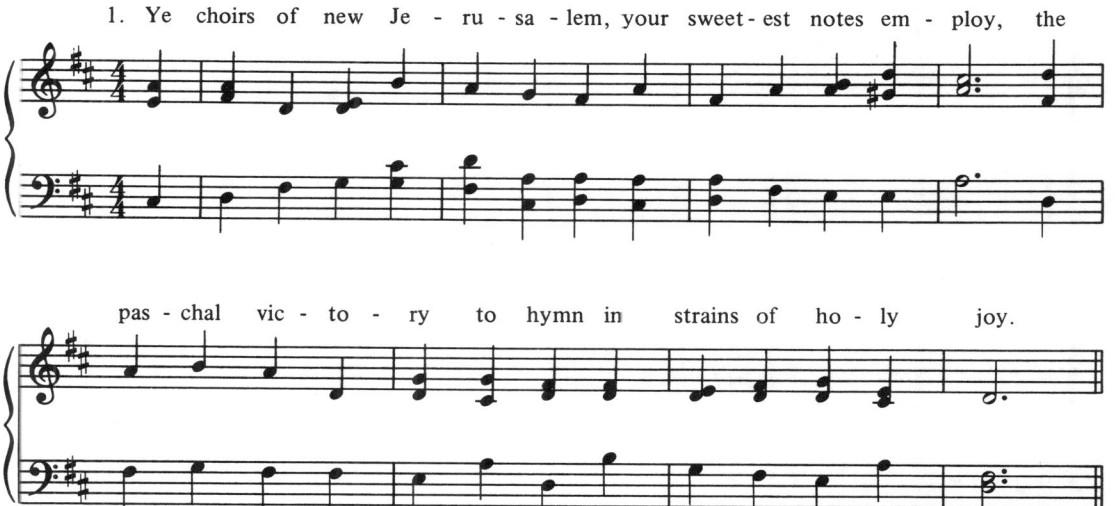

1. Ye choirs of new Je - ru - sa - lem, your sweet - est notes em - ploy, the
pas - chal vic - to - ry to hymn in strains of ho - ly joy.

2. For Judah's Lion bursts his chains,
   crushing the serpent's head;
   and cries aloud through death's domains
   to wake the imprisoned dead.

3. Devouring depths of hell their prey
   at his command restore;
   his ransomed hosts pursue their way
   where Jesus goes before.

4. Triumphant in his glory now
   to him all power is given;
   to him in one communion bow
   all saints in earth and heaven.

5. While we his soldiers praise our King,
   his mercy we implore,
   within his palace bright to bring
   and keep us evermore.

6. All glory to the Father be,
   all glory to the Son,
   all glory, Holy Ghost, to thee,
   while endless ages run.

ST FULBERT C.M.

Text: St Fulbert of Chartres (*d.* 1028), translated by Robert Campbell (1814-1868)
Music: Henry John Gauntlett (1805-1876)

99 Ye holy angels bright

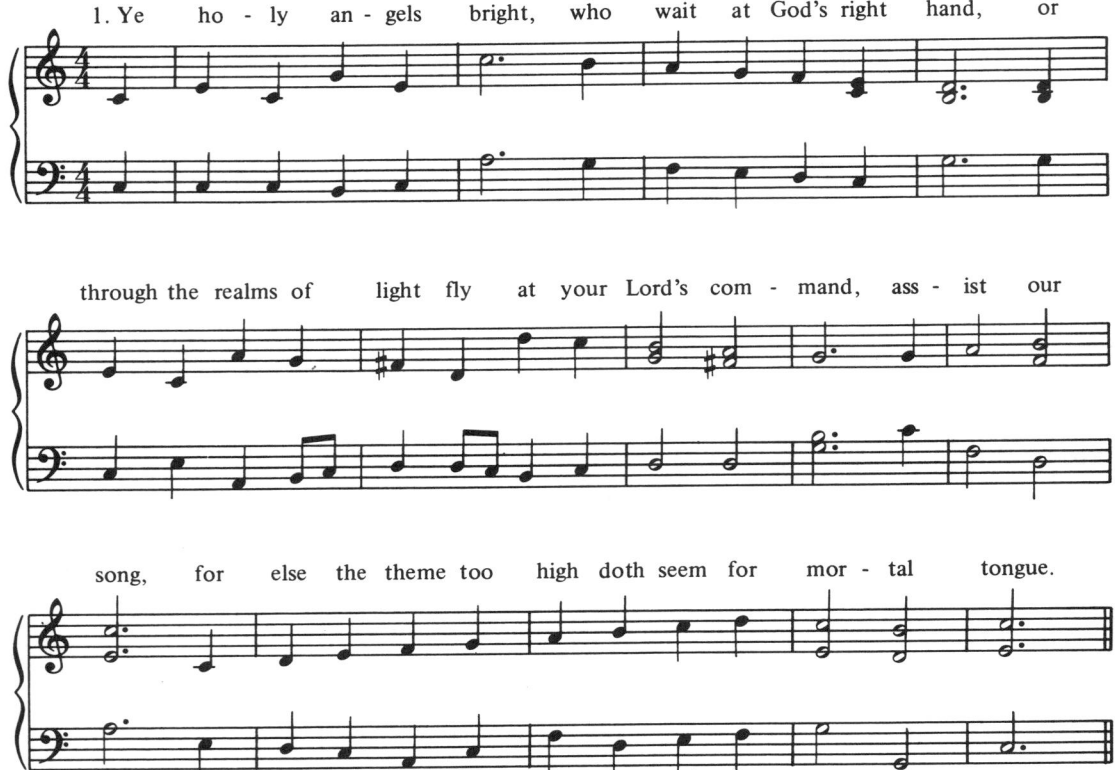

1. Ye holy angels bright, who wait at God's right hand, or through the realms of light fly at your Lord's command, assist our song, for else the theme too high doth seem for mortal tongue.

2. Ye blessed souls at rest,
who ran this earthly race,
and now, from sin released,
behold the Saviour's face,
his praises sound,
as in his light
with sweet delight
ye do abound.

3. Ye saints, who toil below,
adore your heavenly King,
and onward as ye go
some joyful anthem sing;
take what he gives
and praise him still,
through good and ill,
who ever lives.

4. My soul, bear thou thy part,
triumph in God above,
and with a well-tuned heart
sing thou the songs of love;
let all thy days
till life shall end,
whate'er he send,
be filled with praise.

DARWALL'S 148th 6 6. 6 6. 4 4. 4 4.
Text: Richard Baxter (1615-1691) and John Hampden Gurney (1802-1862)
Music: John Darwall (1731-1789)

100 Ye servants of God

1. Ye ser-vants of God, your mas-ter pro-claim, and pub-lish a-broad his won-der-ful name; the name all vic-tor-ious of Je-sus ex-tol; his king-dom is glo-rious, and rules ov-er all.

2. God ruleth on high, almighty to save;
   and still he is nigh: his presence we have;
   the great congregation his triumph shall sing,
   ascribing salvation to Jesus our King.

3. Salvation to God who sits on the throne!
   let all cry aloud, and honour the Son.
   The praises of Jesus the angels proclaim,
   fall down on their faces, and worship the Lamb.

4. Then let us adore, and give him his right:
   all glory and power, all wisdom and might,
   and honour and blessing, with angels above,
   and thanks never-ceasing, and infinite love.

PADERBORN 10 10. 11 11.
Text: Charles Wesley (1707-1788) Music: Melody from *Paderborn Gesangbuch* (1765)

101 As the deer

Flowing

1. As the deer pants for the wa-ter, so my soul longs af-ter you.

D   A   Bm(G)   G   Em   A⁷   D

You a-lone are my heart's de-sire and I long to wor-ship you.

A⁷   Bm(G)   G   Em   A⁷   D

Refrain

You a-lone are my strength, my shield, to you a-lone may my spi-rit yield.

Bm(D)   G   D   G   Em   F♯(D)

You a-lone are my heart's de-sire and I long to wor-ship you.

D   A   Bm(G)   G   Em   A⁷   D

2. I want you more than gold or silver,
   only you can satisfy.
   You alone are the real joy-giver
   and the apple of my eye.

3. You're my friend and you're my brother,
   even though you are a king.
   I love you more than any other,
   so much more than anything.

Words and music: Martin Nystrom

102 Be still, for the presence of the Lord

Reverently

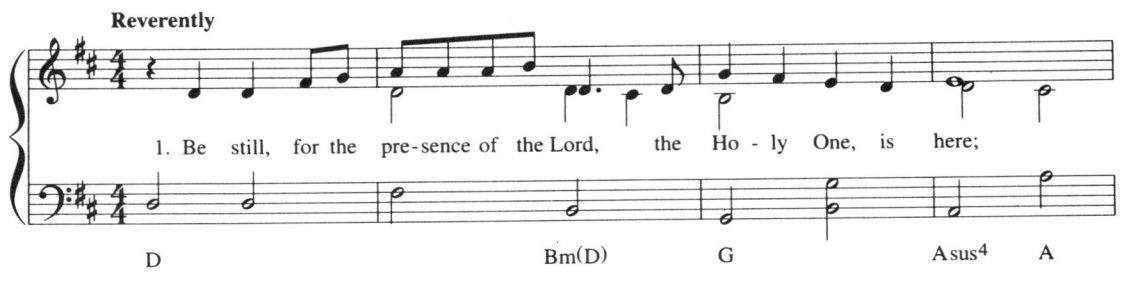

1. Be still, for the pre-sence of the Lord, the Ho-ly One, is here;

D   Bm(D)   G   Asus⁴   A

come bow be-fore him now with re-ve-rence and fear;

D   Bm(D)   G   Asus⁴   A

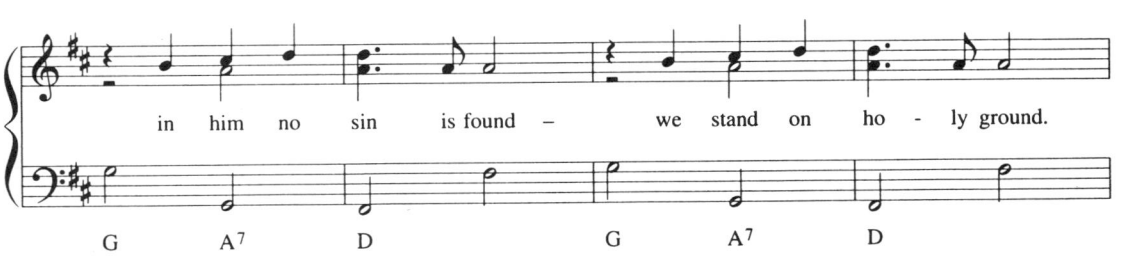

in him no sin is found – we stand on ho-ly ground.

G   A⁷   D   G   A⁷   D

Be still, for the pre-sence of the Lord, the Ho-ly One, is here.

G   A⁷   D   Bm(D)   Em   A⁷   D

2. Be still, for the glory of the Lord is shining all around;
   he burns with holy fire, with splendour he is crowned.
   How awesome is the sight, our radiant king of light!
   Be still, for the glory of the Lord is shining all around.

3. Be still, for the power of the Lord is moving in this place,
   he comes to cleanse and heal, to minister his grace.
   No work too hard for him, in faith receive from him;
   be still, for the power of the Lord is moving in this place.

Words and music: David Evans

103 From heaven you came *(The Servant King)*

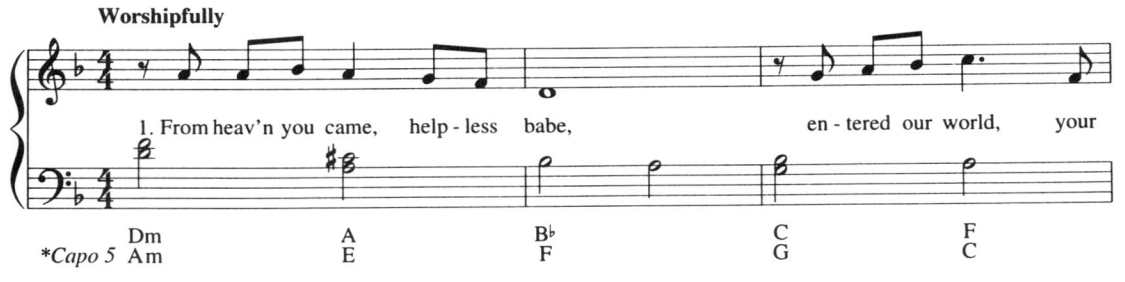

Worshipfully

1. From heav'n you came, help-less babe, en - tered our world, your

Dm   A   B♭   C   F
Capo 5 Am   E   F   G   C

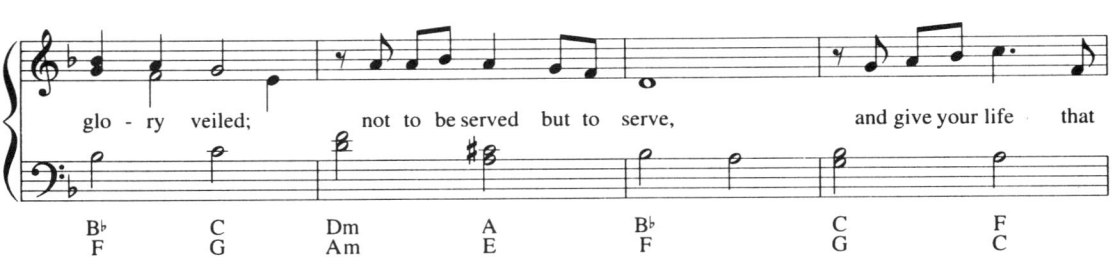

glo - ry veiled; not to be served but to serve, and give your life that

B♭   C   Dm   A   B♭   C   F
F   G   Am   E   F   G   C

Refrain

we might live. This is our God, the Ser-vant King, he calls us

B♭   C   F   C   Dm   F
F   G   C   G   Am   C

now to fol - low him, to bring our lives as a dai-ly of-fer -

Gm   B♭   F   C   F
Dm   F   C   G   C

* Alternative capo chords for guitar

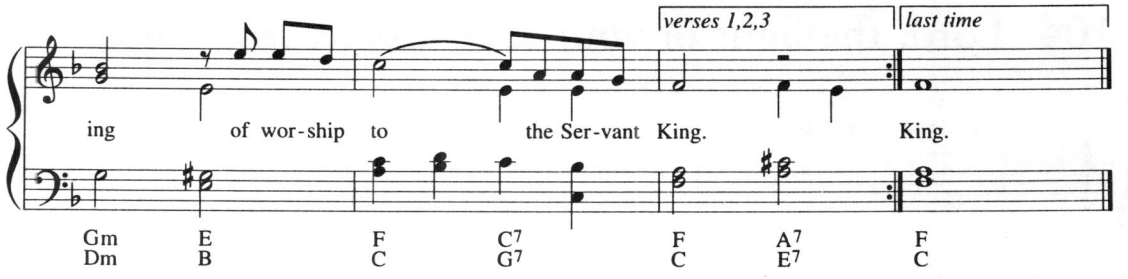

ing   of wor-ship to   the Ser-vant King.   King.

| Gm | E | F | C[7] | F | A[7] | F |
| Dm | B | C | G[7] | C | E[7] | C |

2. There in the garden
   of tears,
   my heavy load
   he chose to bear;
   his heart with sorrow
   was torn,
   'Yet not my will
   but yours', he said.

3. Come see his hands
   and his feet,
   and scars that speak
   of sacrifice,
   hands that flung stars
   into space
   to cruel nails
   surrendered.

4. So let us learn
   how to serve,
   and in our lives
   enthrone him;
   each other's needs
   to prefer,
   for it is Christ
   we're serving.

Words and music: Graham Kendrick

104 Lord, the light of your love *(Shine, Jesus, Shine)*

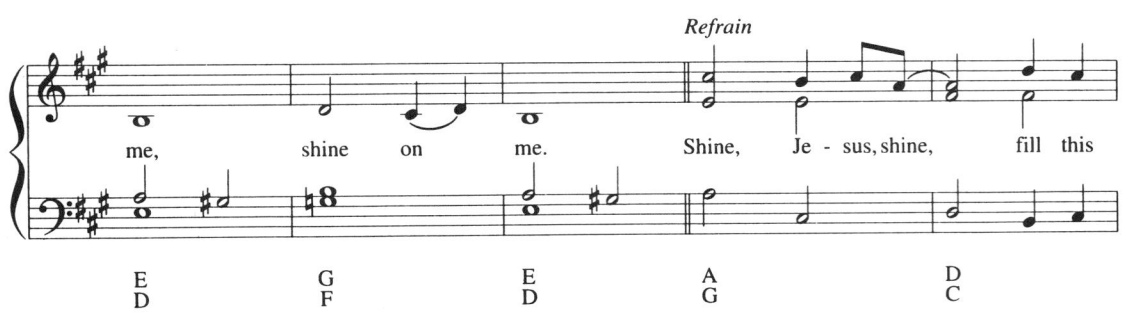

*Alternative capo chords for guitar

land with the Fa-ther's glo-ry; blaze, Spi-rit, blaze, set our hearts on

| Bm | | E | E⁷ | A | | D | Bm |
| Am | | D | D⁷ | G | | C | Am |

fire. Flow, ri-ver, flow, flood the na - tions with grace and mer-cy;

| G | E | A | | D | Bm | | E | E⁷ |
| F | D | G | | C | Am | | D | D⁷ |

D.S. | last time

send forth your word, Lord, and let there be light!

| A | | D | Bm | E⁷ | A | D | A |
| G | | C | Am | D⁷ | G | C | G |

2. Lord, I come to your awesome presence.
from the shadows into your radiance;
by the blood I may enter your brightness,
search me, try me, consume all my darkness,
shine on me, shine on me.

3. As we gaze on your kingly brightness
so our faces display your likeness,
ever changing from glory to glory,
mirrored here may our lives tell your story,
shine on me, shine on me.

Words and music: Graham Kendrick

Index of Uses

Index of Hymn Tunes